Messianic Judaism Class

Student Book

Rabbi Jim Appel
With Jonathan Bernis
and David Levine

OlivePress
צהר זית
Messianic & Christian Publisher

Published by
Olive Press צהר זית
Messianic and Christian Publisher

7267 Lighthouse Rd
Henderson, NY 13650

Messianic & Christian Publisher

Our prayer at Olive Press is that we may help make the Word of Adonai fully known, that it spread rapidly and be glorified everywhere. We hope our books help open people's eyes so they will turn from darkness to Light and from the power of the adversary to God and to trust in ישוע Yeshua (Jesus). (From II Thess. 3:1; Col. 1:25; Acts 26:18,15 NRSV and CJB, the *Complete Jewish Bible*) May this book in particular help reveal the deep meaning in the Jewish roots of our faith.

In honor to God, pronouns referring to the Trinity are capitalized, satan's names are not. Not all Scripture translations do this and legally must be printed as they are.

www.olivepresspublisher.org

Cover and interior design by Olive Press Publisher.
Cover photos by Elisabeth Adams and Cheryl Zehr

Printed in the USA
ISBN 978-0-9847111-3-0
1. Religion: Messianic Judaism 2. Social Science: Jewish Studies 3. Religion: Jewish Holidays

MESSIANIC JUDAISM STUDENT BOOK

All scriptures, unless otherwise indicated, are taken from the *Complete Jewish Bible*. Copyright © 1998 by David H. Stern. Published by Jewish New Testament Publications, Inc. All rights reserved.

Scriptures marked:

NASB are taken from the *New American Standard Bible*. Copyright © 1960, 1962, 1968, 1971, 1972, 1973, 1975, 1977, 1995 by The Lockman Foundation, La Habra, California. All rights reserved.

NIV are taken from the *Holy Bible, New International Version*. Copyright © 1973, 1978, 1984 by International Bible Society. All rights reserved.

NKJV are taken from the *New King James Version*. Copyright © 1982 by Thomas Nelson, Inc. All rights reserved.

TLB are taken from *The Living Bible*. Copyright © 1971 by Tyndale House Publishers, Inc. Used by permission. All rights reserved.

Table Of Contents

Contents in Detail

Contents in Detail (cont.)

Contents in Detail (cont.)

To our Jewish Messiah

ישוע

May He help you absorb
and retain all this and
get to know Him better
because of it.

INTRODUCTION: What is Messianic Judaism?

It is impossible to understand what Messianic Judaism is without knowing a bit of history.

Scriptural Judaism

Older than and much different from modern Rabbinical Judaism is what this essay will label Scriptural Judaism: how the Torah told the Israelites to be Jewish. It is not a modern division of Judaism. It cannot be practiced today because it relies on animal sacrifices. Leviticus 17:8-9 has prohibited these since the Second Temple was destroyed in the year 70 CE.* So there are no Scriptural Jewish congregations today. There are only rabbinical Jewish congregations and Messianic Jewish congregations.

The Judaism of Yeshua's day was Scriptural Judaism. It was augmented by much rabbinical teaching, but its focus was on the Temple and its rituals and sacrifices.

Judaism Divides

In the year 70 CE* the Second Temple was destroyed. It was no longer possible to practice Scriptural Judaism. Without the Temple sacrifices to atone for their sins, what would the Jewish people do?

At that time there were many sects of Judaism: Pharisees, Sadducees, Essenes, Zealots, Nazarenes. All of these were different ways of augmenting Scriptural Judaism with other teachings. Only two of these sects survived: the Pharisees and the Nazarenes.

The Pharisees became Rabbinical Judaism

One surviving sect was the Pharisees. This sect became Rabbinical Judaism, what today includes Orthodox Judaism, Conservative Judaism, and Reform Judaism. It adapted to the destruction of the Second Temple by adopting the teachings of Rabbi Yochanan ben Zakkai.

"The principal figure at hand, Yochanan ben Zakkai, described in rabbinical writings as Hillel's leading disciple, is represented as the master, the sage and rabbi, whose teachings guided Israel beyond the end [the destruction of the Temple]...Yochanan offered not hope of speedy redemption, but rather a conditional promise: just as punishment surely followed sin [the destruction of the Temple was seen as punishment for Israel relying on arms instead of God when resisting the Romans], so will redemption certainly follow repentance" (Jacob Neusner, *Judaism in the Beginning of Christianity*, pages 89, 93, 94).

Yochanan ben Zakkai developed and popularized the theory of Tikkun Olam: salvation comes by studying Torah and doing acts of kindness that help repair the broken human world.

"Yochanan thought that through "khessed" [lovingkindness] the Jews might make atonement, and that the sacrifices now demanded of them were love and mercy.... Yochanan emphasized the primacy of khessed itself in the redemptive process: Just as the Jews needed a redemptive act of compassion from God, so must they now act compassionately in order to make themselves worthy of it.... The earlier age had stood on the books of the Torah, the Temple rites, and acts of piety. The new age would endure on the foundation of studying the Torah, doing the commandments, and especially performing acts of compassion" (Jacob Neusner, *Judaism in the Beginning of Christianity*, pages 96-97).

Rabbinical Judaism has kept Tikkun Olam as its responsibility and its supposed path to salvation ever since.

The Nazarenes

The Nazarenes were the Jews who believed Yeshua was the Messiah. Acts 21:20 tells that there were "tens of thousands" of Torah-observant Nazarenes in Judea alone.

The Nazarenes adapted to the destruction of the Second Temple with ease. Yeshua's sacrifice meant that the Temple sacrifices were meaningful ways of keeping the covenant of Sinai when the Temple stood, but these sacrifices were no longer necessary for atonement or prerequisites for experiencing the presence of God.

*Common Era. Jews use BCE and CE in place of BC. and AD.

History of Messianic Judaism

For a while, after the destruction of the Second Temple, the Pharisees and Nazarenes co-existed fairly peacefully. Violent confrontations such as those mentioned in the book of Acts happened infrequently as each sect focused on re-defining itself without the Temple rituals and sacrifices. The Jewish population of that day was used to its many sects, and most Pharisees saw the Nazarenes as just another group of deluded people who thought so-and-so was the messiah. Such things happened frequently. It's just a phase.

Chapters ten and eleven of the book of Acts tell how the Nazarenes eventually accepted Gentiles into their faith in the year 41 C.E. There were soon more Gentile than Jewish believers. Friction was produced as Gentile and Jewish cultures encountered each other within the Nazarene community outside of Israel. Division and hostility was created over disagreements over dietary laws, circumcision, and holy days. The Nazarene leadership was initially Jewish, in Jerusalem.

Acts 15 tells of the council of the Jewish leadership making their final decision on the Gentile question. Their answer was to receive the Gentile believers into the fold without requiring circumcision and strict adherence to Torah and the traditions. They decided to allow the Gentiles to learn Torah slowly as they would be hearing it taught every week in the synagogues. Thus Jew and Gentile could continue to worship together.

In 132 C.E., Simeon bar Koziba led the last revolt against the Romans. The Nazarenes were part of the revolt until Rabbi Akiba declared that bar Koziba was the messiah and called him bar Kokhba (son of the Star). Since the Nazarenes could not accept this, they left the revolt. The Pharisees felt betrayed and expelled the Nazarenes from the Jewish community.

Slowly, over the next couple centuries, power among believers shifted to the Gentiles who began to change some Biblical Jewish practices, including keeping Shabbat on the first day of the week instead of the seventh. In the early fourth century, in 325 C.E., the council of Nicea, while doing the right thing of declaring that Messiah is divine, also separated Resurrection Day completely from Passover and from the Jewish calendar. Later, the council of Antioch decreed that anyone celebrating Passover would be excommunicated. This was eventually extended to those observing the Jewish Shabbat. The split between Messianic Jews and Gentile Christians was made official.

During the next century, Messianic Judaism faded away. Jewish believers still existed, but were taken into Gentile society. The idea that someone cannot be both Jewish and believe in Yeshua had taken root; the misunderstandings that support it had been established. For the next 1,600 years, Jewish individuals who believed in Yeshua joined Gentile churches. There seemed to be no other option.

In 1915, some Jewish believers in the U.S. founded the Hebrew Christian Alliance. By 1925, this organization had grown large enough to name itself the International Hebrew Christian Alliance. The members of this group, however, still attended Gentile churches.

In 1948 Israel again became a nation. In 1967 Israel captured Jerusalem during the Six Day War. Yeshua had taught about the "times of the Gentiles."

"...and Jerusalem will be trampled under foot by the Gentiles until the times of the Gentiles be fulfilled" (Luke 21:24).

For the first time in nearly 2,000 years, the Jewish people again controlled Jerusalem. The "times of the Gentiles" had ended. That year Messianic Judaism was reborn. The first congregation in 1,600 years consisting of Jewish people believing in Yeshua, while keeping their Jewish traditions and heritage, was started in Cincinnati.

Today, there are Messianic Synagogues in almost every major city across America. Other nations such as Israel, Canada, England, France, Australia, South Africa, Russia, and the Ukraine are experiencing a growing, thriving movement of Messianic Jews as well. Messianic Judaism grew so quickly that by 2008 there were more than 400 congregations in the U.S. and more than 100 in Israel and by 2012 more than 350,000 Jewish believers worldwide.

Messianic Judaism Today

Messianic Judaism is a movement that gets its motivation from the Spirit of God. It is the rebirth of the ancient Nazarene sect: Jewish people following Yeshua while retaining their Jewish lifestyle, traditions, and culture. It is not a new sect of Christianity. There are a few churches from Christian denominations that have adopted a Messianic Jewish flavor, but in these cases it is them who are joining us. Messianic Judaism has never been Jewish people joining Christianity. There are many people who call themselves "Jewish Christians" who are Jews who have joined Christianity, but that is not Messianic Judaism.

Messianic Judaism is not a denomination. It is not governed by a hierarchy or an organization, as denominations are. It is not defined by its theology, as denominations are. Instead, each congregation is founded as God leads a Jewish believer to start a new congregation. There is an organization (the International Association of Messianic Churches and Synagogues) who ordains these "Messianic rabbis," but the organization serves only to establish the requirements for someone to call themselves a "Messianic rabbi." It does not control the congregations or orchestrate the Messianic Judaism movement.

Messianic Judaism is not the same as the organization named "Jews for Jesus." Jews for Jesus is an organization, not a denomination. The membership of Jews for Jesus includes both Messianic Jews and Jewish Christians.

Scriptural Judaism Today

If you follow either Rabbinical or Messianic Judaism, you might be interested in knowing how a form of Scriptural Judaism survives today.

The Torah has certain commandments which are said to be "for all time" or "for all generations." These commandments are special. Why are they special? There are commandments which require the Temple to be standing with its rituals and sacrifices in place. None of these are "for all time" or "for all generations." There are commandments which require living in Israel. None of these are "for all time" or "for all generations." There are commandments which require adopting an agricultural lifestyle. None of these are "for all time" or "for all generations." There are commandments which require living within an all-Jewish community. None of these are "for all time" or "for all generations."

In other words, God foresaw the destruction of the Temple and the Diaspora. God foresaw how someone living in America today would be trying to live as a Jew. And God highlighted the commandments that should and can be kept no matter where or how you live.

Actually, this should not be a surprise. The Torah ends with God making it quite clear that the Israelites would not obey the commandments, and that God would then scatter the people from the Promised Land.

> *And the Lord said to Moses, "Behold, you are about to lie down with your fathers; and this people will arise and play the harlot with the strange gods of the land, into the midst of which they are going, and will forsake Me and break My covenant which I have made with them. Then My anger will be kindled against them in that day, and I will forsake them and hide My face from them...."*
> -Deuteronomy 31:16-17 (NASB)

> *"Then you shall be left few in number, whereas you were as the stars of heaven for multitude, because you did not obey the Lord your God. And it shall come about that as the Lord delighted over you to prosper you, and multiply you, so the Lord will delight over you to make you perish and destroy you; and you shall be torn from the land where you are entering to possess it. Moreover, the Lord will scatter you among all the people, from one end of the earth to the other end of the earth...."*
> -Deuteronomy 28:62-64 (NASB)

So God, knowing this would happen, labeled certain commandments "for all time" or "for all generations" so that even in Babylonian captivity or in the twentieth century it would be clear what the Torah expects.

Which commandments are "for all time" or "for all generations"? A few are specifically for the descendants of Aaron. The others, for Jewish people in general, are:

- Circumcision (Genesis 17:12)
- Celebrate Shabbat (Exodus 31:16,17)
- Celebrate Passover, Unleavened Bread, Shavuot, Yom Kippur, Rosh Hashanah, and Sukkot (Exodus 12:14,17,24; Leviticus 16:29 and chapter 23)
- Keep the eternal lamp lit (Exodus 27:21)
- Do not eat blood or meat-fat (Leviticus 3:17)
- Wear tassels on the corners of your clothing (Numbers 15:38)
- Gentiles who wish to participate may do so (Numbers 15:15)

Unit One
The Messianic Vision

Definition of the Vision

THE VISION:

Messianic Judaism is a restoration movement of congregations made up of Jews and Gentiles who believe in the Messiah Yeshua (Jesus), and worship the God of Israel in a Jewish way (6/16/2011)

Definition of Individual Words

Restoration

1. How does a restoration movement differ from a new movement?

Movement

2. How does a movement differ from an association or denomination?

Congregation

3. What can congregations do that individuals cannot do?

Jews and Gentiles

4. How does this phrase set us apart from churches and traditional synagogues?

Yeshua

5. What influence does Yeshua have in our activities?

Worship

6. What does worship mean in this context?

In a Jewish way

7. How do we worship in a Jewish way?

Definition of Prophetic Vision in General

Proverbs 29:18 Where there is no vision, the people perish...
> 8. What is the Hebrew word for vision or revelation?

> 9. Is this referring to a literal vision, a mystical experience?

Habakkuk 2:2-3.
> 10. What characteristic of the vision does this verse describe?

Amos 3:3 Do two walk together unless they have agreed to do so?
> 11. How does this verse apply to what we are doing today?

Definition of the Messianic Vision

It's not a literal vision or mystical impartation, not a divine election (exclusive), and not simply Jews who believe in Jesus;

It's a revelation and understanding that leads to personal involvement, not just mental assent.

Five Points of the Messianic Vision

Point One: God Is Faithful

We see God's faithfulness to Israel and the Jewish people and His continued plan for Israel (the people, the land and the state).

Genesis 12:3
> 12. What do we call this promise of God?

> 13. How long will this covenant last?

Leviticus 26:38-45
> 14. What do we learn about the sureness of this covenant from this passage?

> 15. Whose faithfulness does it depend on?

Romans 11:28-29
16. Why is God faithful to Israel?

Jeremiah 31:31-37
17. Who is this covenant with?

18. Which covenant is this new covenant not like?

19. Why was a new covenant needed?

20. What has God done through the New Covenant that enables us to keep it?

Acts 15:8-9
21. Who has been added into this covenant?

Point Two: Our Value and Role
We see the value of the Messianic congregation and its role as a corporate witness to the Jewish people and to the Gentile church.

Hebrews 10:22-25
22. What is the value of the congregation as a witness to the Jewish community and to the church?

Point Three: Harmony and Continuity
A. Harmony Between Being Jewish and Believing in Yeshua

Acts 21:17-25
23. What fraction of the population of Jerusalem did these believers represent?

24. Did Jews in the time of the Book of Acts have a problem with being Jewish and believing in Yeshua?

25. Did they remain faithful to the Laws of Moses?

B. Continuity and Harmony Between the Jewish Bible and the Writings of the Apostles

2 Timothy 3:15-17
26. What Scripture is Paul (Sha'ul in Hebrew) talking about here?

27. What is the foundation for the Apostolic Writings?

Acts 26:14-15
   28. What language did Yeshua speak after He was glorified?

Revelation 5:5
   29. What title of Yeshua indicates that He still identifies with being Jewish?

C. What Does This Harmony and Continuity Say to Gentiles?
Ephesians 3:6
   30. What is the Gentiles' place?

   31. Why did Rabbi Sha'ul use the Greek prefix for "joint" three times rather than just once?

1 Peter 2:5-9
   32. Who is being built into a spiritual house and what is the point of the analogy?

   33. Who is Peter calling the King's cohanim (priests) and a holy nation?

Romans 11:11
   34. What is one of the roles the Gentiles will fulfill?

   35. What has the church provoked Israel to over the past 1700 years?

Isaiah 49:22
   36. What is another role the Gentiles will fulfill?

Point Four: Salvation
Commitment to Yeshua as God's only plan for Salvation

   37. What do some of the liberal churches who engage in dialogue with synagogues accept?

   38. What happens if you accept this belief?

John 14:6
   39. What does this tell us about the two plans for salvation?

John 3:36

    40. Who has eternal life?

    41. Who does not?

Romans 1:16 (NKJV)

    42. What is the Biblical order for the proclamation of the Gospel?

    43. Is this order historically sequential or is it for today? Is it optional?

Point Five: Deep Expectation of End Time Jewish Revival

We believe this Jewish revival will happen soon.

Romans 11:15

    44. What must precede the resurrection of the dead?

    45. When will this resurrection of the dead occur?

Romans 11:26

    46. Is any other nation promised total salvation?

Zechariah 12:1-9

    47. Who are the people surrounding Jerusalem?

    48. What does a "cup that will stagger" mean?

    49. What does it mean "Yerushalayim a heavy stone for all the peoples. All who try to lift it will hurt themselves"?

    50. What nations will be "massed against" Jerusalem?

    51. Who will destroy the nations attacking Jerusalem?

Zechariah 12:10 to 13:1

52. Who will this spirit of grace and prayer be poured out upon?

53. Who will they see?

54. What will their reaction be?

55. What will be the cleansing liquid in the fountain?

Unit Two:
Jewish Lifestyle and Traditions

Shabbat

Exodus 31:13

   1. Why did God command us to keep the Shabbat?

Exodus 31:16

   2. For how long are we to keep the Shabbat?

Exodus 20:8-11

   3. What are we commanded to do and not do on Shabbat?

   4. Who else is to rest?

   5. What does this commandment imply concerning doing things that require other people to work on Shabbat?

   6. What event is the Shabbat a commemoration of?

Deuteronomy 5:15

   7. What other event is the Shabbat a commemoration of?

Nehemiah 13:15

   8. What else are we not to do?

Exodus 35:3
   9. What else are we commanded not to do?

Isaiah 58: 3-14
   10. What should our attitude about the Shabbat be?

Mark 2:27
   11. What does Yeshua mean by this statement?

John 7: 23
   12. Why could a child be circumcised on Shabbat?

Luke 13: 15
   13. What other kind of work is allowed on Shabbat?

Matthew 12:1-5
   14. How and why did the priests desecrate the day?

   15. How does this Scripture apply to the work of the ministry on Shabbat?

Matthew 12:6
   16. What does He mean by this statement?

Matthew 12:7-8
    17. What does He mean by this statement?

Matthew 12:9-11
    18. What work is allowed on Shabbat?

Matthew 12:12-14
    19. Why did the P'rushim (Pharisees) decide to destroy Yeshua?

Leviticus 23:3
    20. What are we to do together on the Shabbat?

    21. How is Shabbat kept by the Orthodox?

    22. How is the Sabbath kept by many Christian groups?

    23. How do we Messianics keep Shabbat?

Isaiah 56:6-7
24. What is God's promise to the Gentiles who keep Shabbat?

Acts 15:28-29
25. What requirements were placed on the Gentile followers of Yeshua?

26. Were there other expectations?

Acts 15:9-10
27. What is the yoke?

Romans 14:5-6
28. To whom is the book of Romans written?

29. What attitude should we have toward those outside the congregation and those inside the congregation who don't keep Shabbat in the same way we do?

Appointed Times — Moadim of the Lord
Biblical Holiday Chart

Modern Hebrew Name	English Name	Ashkenazi Hebrew Name	Biblical Reference
	Passover		Exodus 12 Leviticus 23
	Unleavened Bread		Exodus 12 Leviticus 23
	FirstFruits		Leviticus 23
	Feast of Weeks Pentecost		Leviticus 23
	Feast of Trumpets, Head of the Year, New Year		Leviticus 23
	Day of Atonement		Leviticus 16, 23
	Feast of Tabernacles, Feast of Booths		Leviticus 23
	Feast of the Dedication, Festival of Lights		1&2 Macabees
	Feast of Esther		Esther

The Hebrew word used in Scripture for "Biblical holidays" is "Moadim" which means "Appointed Times." "Moadim" is plural. "Moad" is singular for one "Appointed Time."

Time of Year	Important to	Commemorates	Prophetic Meaning

Appointed Times — Moadim of the Lord (cont.)

PASSOVER — PESAKH

30. What Moadim start on days 14 and 15 of the first Jewish month (Nisan)?

Leviticus 23:5-8

31. What is the Hebrew name for Passover?

32. What is commemorated by Passover?

33. How do we celebrate Passover?

A Traditional Seder

Haggadah

Seder Plate
Karpas

Moror

Kharoset

Haggadah Story Continues

The Plagues

34. Does anyone see a similarity with Pesakh, Chanukah, and Purim?

God's Instructions for Surviving the Tenth Plague

Exodus 12:3

Exodus 12:6-7

Exodus 12:12-13

Exodus 12:29-33

35. What does Pesakh symbolize to Messianic Believers?

Testimony

1 Corinthians 5:7
36. How do we get set free from being in Egypt?

37. Why is He called our Passover Lamb?

38. What pattern did the blood make on the doorposts of the houses?

John 1: 29 (KJV)
John 6:47
39. What are these verses telling us?

40. Why don't most Jewish people eat lamb at Pesakh today?

UNLEAVENED BREAD — KHAG HA MATZAH
41. What is the Hebrew name of the food associated with Unleavened Bread?

Leviticus 23:5-6
Exodus 12:39
42. Why do we eat Matzah?

43. What is commemorated by eating Matzah?

44. What is symbolized by Matzah?

45. How do we celebrate as Messianic Believers?

FIRSTFRUITS — BUKKURIM

Leviticus 23:9-14

46. What is commemorated by Firstfruits?

47. What is the Hebrew name for Firstfruits?

48. When does Firstfruits occur?

1.

2.

3.

Luke 24:1

49. What happened on Firstfruits, the Sunday following Pesakh the year Yeshua was sacrificed?

50. What is symbolized by Firstfruits?

1 Corinthians 15:20-23

Here's the connection with Firstfruits:

Firstfruits is Resurrection Day

51. Why is living with the reality of His Resurrection so important?

First

Second
   A.
   B.

52. Why did the resurrection happen on Firstfruits?

53. How do we celebrate as Messianic Believers?

FEAST OF WEEKS, PENTECOST — SHAVUOT

Leviticus 23:15-21

54. What does Shavuot mean?

55. When do we celebrate Shavuot?

56. What is celebrated on Shavuot according to Leviticus 23?

FEAST OF WEEKS — PENTECOST — SHAVUOT (cont.)

57. What event is associated with Shavuot by the rabbis?

Acts 2:1-4
58. What event is associated with Shavuot in the B'rit Hadashah (New Covenant)?

John 14:26
John 16:13
59. What is God's message to us in these two world-changing events happening on the same day on the Jewish calendar?

60. How do we celebrate as Messianic Believers?

FEAST OF TRUMPETS — ROSH HASHANAH — YOM TERUAH

Leviticus 23:23-25
61. The Biblical Hebrew name is Yom Teruah. What does Yom Teruah mean?

62. What is the traditional name for this holiday?

63. What does Rosh Hashanah mean?

64. What is the traditional way of celebrating this holiday?

New Year's Day:

Traditional Greeting: L'shana Tova. Ti ki tevu:

Traditional Theme:

Ten Days of Awe:

65. How do we celebrate as Messianic Believers?

1 Thessalonians 4:16
66. What is the future prophetic significance of this holiday?

DAY OF ATONEMENT — YOM KIPPUR

Leviticus 23:26-32
   67. What does Yom Kippur mean?

   68. How was Yom Kippur commemorated in the time of the Temple?
Leviticus 16:2,17

Hebrews 9:3-5

Leviticus 16:17

The Two Goats
Leviticus 16:5-9,10
   69. What was the second goat called?

Leviticus 16:21-22
   The scapegoat bore away the iniquity.

Genesis 6:5 (NKJV)
   70. What is iniquity?
   Khatahah
   Pesha
   Avone

Isaiah 59:1-2 (NKJV)

Isaiah 53:5-6 (NKJV)
   71. What is the Messianic Significance of the scapegoat?

Leviticus 16:22 (NASB)
   72. What is the Messianic significance of this part of the ceremony?

   73. How do we celebrate Yom Kippur as a Messianic Congregation?

FEAST OF TABERNACLES—SUKKOT

Leviticus 23:33-44

74. What does Sukkot mean?

75. What are some English names for this holiday?

76. How do we celebrate Sukkot?

77. What meaning do these observations have?

A. Harvest Festival

B. Z'man Simkhatenu (The Time of Our Rejoicing)

C. Living in Booths or Sukkot — Temporary Dwellings

D. Future Messianic, Prophetic Meaning

78. What future event is associated with this holiday?

Zechariah 14:3

79. Who will defend Yerushalayim (Jerusalem)?

Zechariah 14:9

80. What is this verse saying?

Zechariah 14:16-17

81. What can we ascertain from this that will happen in the Millennial Kingdom?

Two Fascinating Connections to Yeshua Coming to Earth the First Time.

First Connection: A Past Messianic Prophetic Meaning

82. What event in Yeshua's life is associated with this holiday?

83. What Holy Day in the seventh month would have been appropriate for the day of His birth?

84. Why?

85. Why else?

Second Connection: A Future Messianic Prophetic Meaning

John 7:2,10
86. What did Yeshua do on Sukkot?

87. How was the last day of Sukkot celebrated in the time of the Temple?
The Water Drawing Ceremony

Hoshiana Rabbah

Springs of Salvation

John 7:37

88. What did Yeshua declare for all to hear on this holiday?

89. What was Yeshua saying and why did He choose to say it on Sukkot?

John 7:38

John 7:39

John 4:14

90. Why a river?

91. Why plural as in "rivers"?

92. So, if we're supposed to have *"rivers of living water flow from our inmost beings"*, how do we keep them flowing?

93. How do we let the rivers flow out?

94. What else is needed to keep them flowing out?

95. How do we let them in?

96. How we observe this Moad (Appointed Time) today.

John 7:37 "If anyone is thirsty, let him keep coming to me and drinking!…
97. Does being filled with the Ruakh HaKodesh happen just once and then we're filled forever?

SIMCHA TORAH (Rejoicing in the Torah)

98. What does this day celebrate?

99. How do we celebrate?

100. When do we celebrate it?

Nehemiah 8:18
101. What is the origin of Simcha Torah?

102. What is the significance of this holiday?

103. What is the importance of Simcha Torah?

John 1:14
    104. What is the descriptor of the Word that the Scripture uses about itself?

Deuteronomy 16:16
    105.. Which holidays are the three pilgrimage holidays ?

    106. What is the significance of this?

Historical Holidays
HANUKKAH, Feast of Dedication, Feast of Lights
(Maccabees and John 10:22)
107. What is Hanukkah all about?

108. How is it celebrated in Judaism today?

Galatians 4:4 (NKJV)
109. Why does Hanukkah have much more importance to believers?

110. Could Yeshua have been without defect or spot, without sin, under the law if the Hellenization of Israel had succeeded?

111. What did Yeshua teach during this holiday?

Christmas
Our congregation celebrates **Erev Yom HaMashiach (Day of the Messiah)** on Christmas Eve. We always teach on Yeshua's birth on the Shabbat closest to Christmas day, although we believe He was born on Sukkot. Many intermarried families celebrate at home.

PURIM (Esther)

112. What event is celebrated?

113. What are some of the historical details concerning this incident?

Esther 3:4-6
114. Why would a villain want to wipe out all the Jewish people?

115. How do we get the name "Purim" for this holiday?

Esther 3:13
Imagine the fear, anguish these letters brought!

Mordecai begged Queen Esther to intercede with the King to save the Jewish people.
Esther replied to Mordecai
Esther 4:11

Mordecai answered Esther
Esther 4:13-14

What a man of faith Mordecai was.

Esther answered:
Esther 4:16

Esther had survived the test.
Esther 5:3

She invited the king and Haman to two banquets. At the second banquet Queen Esther finally
spoke up.
Esther 7:3-6

116. How is Purim celebrated?

117. What would have happened if Haman had succeeded?

Modern Historical Remembrance Days

118. What three modern historical holidays are celebrated in the spring very close together?

Yom Ha Shoah (Day of the Holocaust) Nissan 27

119. Why is it important to commemorate this terrible event?

Yom Ha Zikaron (Israel's Remembrance Day) Iyar 4

120. What is remembered on this day?

121. How is this day commemorated?

Yom Ha Atzmaut (Israel Independence Day) Iyar 5

122. What is the Biblical significance of this event?

Tisha B'Av (The Ninth of the Month of Av)

123. What is this holiday about?

124. How do we commemorate this day?

Biblical Laws
Kashrut (Keeping Kosher)

Leviticus 11: 2-8
125. What is the test for a kosher animal?

Leviticus 11:9-12
126. What is the test for a kosher fish?

Leviticus 11:13-19
127. Is there a test for kosher birds?

128. What kinds of birds are listed here?

Leviticus 11:20-23
129. What is the test for a kosher insect?

130. What is the difference between keeping Biblical Kosher and traditional Kosher?

131. Are there different levels of strictness in keeping kosher?

Deuteronomy 14:21
132. Can you have milk and meat together in the same meal?

Kosher for Passover
133. What's the reason for special Passover kosher?

Food Laws in the New Covenant

Acts 10:10-16
> Anti-nomian (free grace) theology has interpreted this to say the New Covenant has overturned the Torah food laws and therefore also all other "Jewish" laws. Let's check to see if that is true.

Acts 10:28
> 134. What was Peter's interpretation of the vision?

> 135. What did Peter mean when he said it's "something that just isn't done (CJB), "unlawful" (NKJV)"?

> 136. Was it a law of God that kept Jews from interacting with Gentiles?
>   If so, where is it in the Scriptures?

Mark 7:1-23
> 137. What was the issue in this passage?

Acts 15: 28-29
> 138. What dietary requirements have been placed on the Gentiles?

> 139. Why keep the Kosher laws?

As Messianics, we need to apply "Hallakhah" to the Kosher laws
> 140. What is the hallakhah hierarchy of the Kosher laws?

Acts 28: 17
> 141. Did Paul keep the law and the Jewish traditions?

> 142. So, what kinds of food can you bring to Messianic Congregation events?

Prayer Shawl — Tallit/Tallis; Tassels — Tzit-Tzit

Numbers 15: 38-40

143. What is the purpose of the tzit-tzit (tassels or fringes)?

144. How long is this command to be obeyed?

145. How do Jewish people fulfill this commandment?

146. Where is the Tallit to be worn?

147. Do Messianics follow this law?

148. Are there references to men wearing the tzit-tzit in the Bible?

Malachi 4:2

149. What role does the Tallit have in this prediction about the life of the Messiah?

Mark 6:56

150. Did Yeshua wear a Tallit?

151. What happened to the blue thread?

152. What can this mean except the soon return of Messiah?!

Bar/Bat/B'nei Mitzvah

153. What is the meaning of the words "Bar/Bat Mitsvah"?

154. Why "Bar" instead of "Ben"?

155. When was the first Bat Mitzvah?

156. Is this custom a Biblical command?

157. What's the age for boys? For girls?

158. Is there a Bar Mitzvah reference in the Bible?

159. What meaning does it hold for the person?

160. What's the meaning for the congregation?

161. Can adults be Bar Mitzvah-ed?

162. Is there any other importance?

Baby Dedication
Leviticus 12:3-8

Pidyon haBen—Redemption of the First-born:
Exodus 13:12-15

Luke 2:22-23

Circumcision — B'rit-Milah

Genesis 17: 10-11
163. Why were the babies to be circumcised?

Genesis 17:12
164. Who is to be circumcised?

165. When are they to be circumcised?

Genesis 17:13
166. How long is this covenant to last?

Genesis 17:14
167. How important does God consider circumcision?

168. What is a person who performs circumcisions called?

169. Are there any physical benefits to circumcision?

170. Can you think of any periods in Biblical and Jewish history when this covenant was ignored?

171. Is circumcision referred to in the B'rit Hadashah?

At our congregation, we strongly encourage if either parent is Jewish to bring the child into the Abrahamic covenant. For Gentiles, circumcision is not required or encouraged.

1 Corinthians 7:17-20
172. Should non-Jewish baby boys be circumcised?

Kippot/Yarmulkes
173. Is there a Biblical basis?

174. What is the reason for wearing them?

175. Do Messianics wear them?

V'ahavtah, T'fillen, Mezuzah

Deuteronomy 6:4"
> 176. What is the significance of this verse?

V'ahavtah

Deuteronomy 6:6-8 is called the V'ahavtah which means "and you shall love."

Deuteronomy 6:5 (NKJV)
> 177. What kind of a relationship does this verse tell us God wants with us?

> 178. What do the words "with all your heart, all your soul, and all your strength" imply about God's intention for His relationship with us?

Deuteronomy 6:6 (NKJV)
> 179. What does it meant that His words should be in our hearts?

Deuteronomy 6:7 (NKJV)
> 180. Why does Moses use the word "diligently" in describing how we should teach our children?

> 181. What if your children have already grown up?

> 182. Why are we given this long list of when we should talk about the Words of God?

Deuteronomy 6:8 (NKJV)
> **T'fillin (Tefillin)** (also called phylacteries)

Deuteronomy 6:9 (NKJV)
> **Mezuzah**

T'vilah, Mikveh, Immersion

IMMERSION IN THE TENAKH

183. Is immersion a Jewish practice?

Exodus 29:1,4
184. What is immersion for in this Exodus passage?

Leviticus 17:15
185. What is immersion for in this Leviticus passage?

Psalm 51:2 (NKJV)
186. Washing or Immersion is an outward sign of what?

IMMERSION IN THE B'RIT HADASHAH

Matthew 3:4-6
187. Why were people coming to Yochanon for immersion?

John 1:24-25
188. Who recognized immersion as a Jewish practice?

189. Whose arrival was immersion associated with by the Jewish people?

Acts 2:38
190. What did Kefa (Peter) instruct the new Jewish believers in Yeshua to do?

191. What does it mean to be immersed on the authority of Yeshua the Messiah into forgiveness of your sins?

192. What has to happen before immersion?

193. What were they promised if they obeyed?

194. Is Kefa's instruction valid for today?

Acts 10:45-48
   195. What issue were the Jewish believers struggling with?

   196. What was their conclusion?

   197. What was the first thing the Jewish believers told the new Gentile believers to do?

   198. Why?

   199. What does it mean to be immersed in the Name of Yeshua, the Messiah?

   200. Why has the practice lost its Jewishness?

   201. Is immersion practiced today in traditional Judaism?

YESHUA AND IMMERSION

Matthew 3:13-14
   202. Why did Yochanan say he ought to be immersed by Yeshua instead of Yeshua
        being immersed by him?

Matthew 3:15
   203. What did Yeshua mean by "because we should do everything righteousness requires"?

Matthew 3:16-17
   204. What phase of Yeshua's life was about to begin at this time?

   205. What application does this passage have to our ministry or lifestyle of serving God?

Mark 16:16
   206. Why are Yeshua's followers to be immersed?

   207. What has to happen before immersion?

Matthew 28:19-20

    208. What else has to happen before immersion?

    209. What does it mean to be immersed into the reality of the Father, the Son and the Ruach HaKodesh?

    210. What is this passage called?

THE MEANING OF IMMERSION IN OUR LIVES

Romans 6:3-5

    211. What does going under the water symbolize?

    212. What does coming up out of the water symbolize?

    213. What is the connection between this idea of death by water and the history of ancient Israel?

Romans 6:6-7

    214. What is the "body of our sinful propensities"?

    215. What happens to our "old self," the "old nature"?

    216. What are we set free from?

Romans 6:8

    217. How does this verse relate to verse. 5?

Romans 6:9-11

    218. What does "in the same way" refer to here?

Romans 6:12
219. What word is understood here?

220. Why does it take exertion to have a victory over sin?

221. What attitude should you have if you've resisted sin in the past and failed?

Romans 6:13
222. What practical advice is there in this verse?

223. Should you wait until you have victory over all your sins before starting to serve?

Romans 6:14
224. Why does sin no longer have authority?

225. What great promise is in this verse?

226. What is the origin of the word "baptize" and what does it mean?

Acts 2:38
227. What must happen before immersion?

228. What implication do these passages have for the custom of infant immersion?

229. What should you do if you were immersed or sprinkled as an infant?

230. What should you do if you were sprinkled as a believing adult?

231. What should you do if you have been immersed before as a believer but you understand it differently now?

S'udat Adonai — The Lord's Table — Communion

Luke 22:19 -20
232. What do the matzah and grape juice (or wine) represent?

233. What is the connection to Pesakh?

1 Corinthians 11:23-25
234. How often are we supposed to partake in S'udat Adonai?

1 Corinthians 11:26
235. What does it mean to proclaim the Lord's death?

Colossians 2:14-15
236. Who are we proclaiming His death to?

1 Corinthians 11:27
237. How can you eat or drink in an unworthy manner?

1 Corinthians 11:28-29
238. What does it mean to "recognize the body"?

1 Corinthians 11:30
239. What are the consequences of eating or drinking in an unworthy manner?

1 Corinthians 11:31-32
240. What inner processes should be occurring during S'udat Adonai?

Unit Three:

Jewish Evangelism,

One on One

Jewish Evangelism, One on One by Rabbi Jim Appel
(6/22/2011)

*Matthew 23:39 For I tell you, from now on, you will not see me again until you say,
`Blessed is he who comes in the name of ADONAI (the Lord).'"*

1. Why Jewish people?

2. Why is special training needed?

We get our structure for this teaching from this passage:

*Colossians 4:3-6 Include prayer for us, too, that God may open a door for us to pro-
claim the message about the secret of the Messiah—for that is why I am in prison.
4 And pray that I may speak, as I should, in a way that makes the message clear. 5
Behave wisely toward outsiders, making full use of every opportunity—6 let your conversation always be gracious and interesting, so that you will know how to respond
to any particular individual.*

I. What Opens a Door?

*Colossians 4:3 Include prayer for us, too, that God may <u>open a door</u> for us to proclaim
the message about the secret of the Messiah ....*

A. Prayer and Faith Open a Door

3. Why should I pray for my Jewish friend's salvation?

1 Timothy 2:3-4
4. Why can I have faith for my friend to come to the knowledge of the truth?

Mark 11:24
5. What does faith do?

Luke 21:24
6. Has this prophesy been fulfilled yet?

2 Corinthians 3:14-16

7. What should I pray for?
   (A list of eleven or so items)

8. Should I tell my friend I'm praying for him?

B. Listening and understanding Open a Door for People to Listen to You

Colossians 4:6 ... let your conversation always be gracious and interesting ....

9. What are some common Jewish ways of thinking we need to understand?
   (A list of at least fourteen items)

10. What are some other Jewish sensitivities?

11. Are there any misconceptions Christians have about Jewish people that hinder evangelism?

12. My Jewish friend knows Scripture better than I do. True or false?

13. If I were Jewish I would be better able to witness. True or false?

14. All Jewish people believe in God like orthodox Jews. True or false?

15. What are the eleven or so different levels of Jewish religious views?

16. What are Jewish people seeking?

C. Inoffensive Terminology Opens a Door

Colossians 4:4 And pray that I may speak, as I should, in a way that makes the message clear.

17. What are some terms that are misunderstood or offensive to Jewish people and how do we correct them?

    Fill this chart in and use it to help you avoid offensive terms.

USE	DON'T USE
	Church
	Jesus
	Christ
	Pastor, Minister, Priest, Father, Reverend
	Jewish Christian, Hebrew Christian, Completed Jew, Converted Jew
	Christian
	Saved, converted, born-again
	Bible, Holy Bible, Word of God
	Old Testament
	Sabbath
	Passover
	Pentecost
	Tabernacles, Booths
	New Testament
	Communion
	Baptism
	Holy Spirit, Holy Ghost
	Gospel
	Missions
	Missionary
	Yahweh, Jehovah

D. Love Opens a Door

Colossians 4:5 Be wise in the way you act toward outsiders.

Relationship
18. How do you show love in your relationship with your Jewish friend?

Commitment
19. Why is commitment important?

Patience
20. Why do we need patience?

Wisdom
21. What part does wisdom play?

E. Hospitality Opens a Door

22. How does one show hospitality?

II. How can I start a conversation about spiritual things?

Colossians 4:5 ... making full use of every opportunity ....

A. Steer the Conversation in That Direction

23. What are some specific conversation starters?

24. What are some spiritual subjects you could talk about?

25. What are some personal spiritual things you could say?

B. Give Witness to the Authenticity of the Bible

Accurate Description of Man

26. Which Scripture best shows this?

Already Fulfilled Prophesy

Deuteronomy 28:62, 64

Leviticus 26:44

Isaiah 11:11-12

Isaiah 35:1

Zechariah 12:2-3

Messianic Prophecies

Micah 5:2

Daniel 9:24-25

Isaiah 7:14

Isaiah 9:6-7

Psalm 22

Isaiah 53:5-7

Zechariah 12:10

Jeremiah 31:31-34

C. Bring Him/Her to a Messianic Synagogue for Shabbat or Holiday Services

27. What is one reason for this?

D. Give Some Encouraging Words About the Gospel

28. What are some encouraging things you could say?

III. How Can I Present the Gospel?

Colossians 4:4 ... that I may speak ... in a way that makes the message clear ....

A. The Way of the Master Technique (with the "Good Person" Test)
www.wayofthemaster.com

Statistics show that of those who come forward at evangelistic meetings
only 5% are regularly attending after one year.
Many blame poor follow up.
The real reason is the wrong motivation for giving their heart to the Lord.
Today the Gospel is often presented as a remedy to fix your life:
Get off drugs, find prosperity, happiness, healing, acceptance, love, purpose, etc.
The Gospel leads to all those things but they shouldn't be
the motivation to make a commitment to the Lord.
Why?
Because we all know satan goes after new believers with great ferocity
and can make their lives worse than before they came to the Lord.
When he does, most fall away concluding that what they were promised was a lie
and it didn't work.

29. What should be the motivation for people to come to the Lord?

30. When the Good News of Messiah taking the penalty they deserve upon Himself is presented, what happens?

31. How do we bring people into the Kingdom with this motivation?

32. What is the sentence to help you remember the five questions to the "Good Person" Test?

Take the test yourself here: www.areyouagoodperson.org

33. How do people usually answer these "Good Person" questions?

▶ Would you consider yourself a <u>good</u> person?

▶ Do you <u>keep</u> the Ten Commandments?

Do you mean you've always put God first in your life?
Do you mean you've never used God's name in a disrespectful way?
Do you mean you've always kept the Sabbath?
Do you mean you've always honored your parents?
Do you mean you've never told a lie?
Do you mean you've never stolen anything?
Do you mean you've never coveted what someone else owns?

Give them Yeshua's interpretation of three others:
- Do you mean you've never committed adultery?
    Matthew 5:28 - Yeshua said if you've lusted after someone
        You've committed adultery in your heart
    Do you mean you've never lusted after someone?

- Do you mean you've never committed murder?
    Matthew 5:22 - Yeshua said if you've hated anyone
        you're guilty of murder in your heart
    Do you mean you've never hated anyone?
- Do you mean you've never worshipped an idol?
    Matthew 6:24 - Yeshua said you can't serve two masters:
        God and earthly things.
    Do you mean nothing has been more important to you than God?

If they admit to any of these, ask the corresponding question:
- Lying: What does that make you? A liar.
- Stealing: What does that make you? A thief.
- Using God's name disrespectfully: What? A blasphemer.
- Lusting: An adulterer.
- Hating: A murderer.

Get them to admit, "I am a liar, thief, adulterer, blasphemer, idolater, Sabbath breaker, coveter, murderer, disrespecter of parents."

▶   If you were to be <u>judged</u> according to the Ten Commandments would you be innocent or guilty?

▶   What would your eternal <u>destiny</u> be, heaven or hell?

▶   Does that <u>concern</u> you?

34. What should you say next if they are concerned about their eternal destiny?

* (If the person is not Jewish skip to the asterisk * after question #37 on the next page.)
   (Continue on if the person is Jewish.)

B. Explain the Gospel From the Tenakh

Leviticus 17:11 For the life of a creature is in the blood, and I have given it to you on the altar to make atonement for yourselves; for it is the blood that makes atonement because of the life.

> When God gave Israel the Ten Commandments He also gave them a way to pay the penalty when they violated the commandments.
>
> According to the Laws of Moses, a person needed to do t'shuvah (be truly repentant, turning away from sin to God) and needed to offer an animal sacrifice whose shed blood would make atonement for (cover over) their sin.

35. How long was this system of atonement through animal sacrifice in place?

Hebrews 9:22 Without the shedding of blood there is no forgiveness of sins.

Leviticus 17:8-9 Also tell them, "When someone from the community of Isra'el or one of the foreigners living with you offers a burnt offering or sacrifice 9 without bringing it to the entrance of the tent of meeting to sacrifice it to ADONAI, that person is to be cut off from his people."

> Since 70 CE the shedding of the blood of animals to make atonement is forbidden because the Temple is no longer standing.

36. What should you point out to him/her about Traditional Judaism?

37. What should you say about that?

* *Isaiah 53:6 (KJV) All we like sheep have gone astray; We have turned, every one, to his own way; And the LORD has laid on Him the iniquity of us all.*
  Isaiah 59:2 (NIV) But your iniquities have separated you from your God ....

> [The above two Tenakh passages correspond to the following two Brit Hadashah ones. Use only if it seems appropriate—only if the Ruakh is leading you to do so:
> *Romans 6:23 (NIV) For the wages of sin is death, but the gift of God is eternal life ...*
>   (By "eternal life" the Scriptures mean life with God.)
> *Romans 3:23 (NIV) for all have sinned and fall short of the glory of God.*]

The Scriptures teach that before the Temple was destroyed Yeshua died as the final sacrifice of the sacrificial system.

He died to pay the penalty for sin to make a way for us to come close to God.

38. How can we receive Yeshua's atoning sacrifice to pay for our sins?

> Lead the person in prayer asking forgiveness, putting their trust in Messiah's atoning sacrifice, committing to obey Yeshua as Lord, thanking God for raising Messiah from the dead.

IV. Tearing Down the Three Walls Blocking the Gospel

Colossians 4:5,6 (NIV) Be wise .... Let your conversation be always full of grace, seasoned with salt ....

A. Wall of Replacement Theology

39. What is the wall of Replacement Theology?

40. But true Christians wouldn't persecute or hate Jews, would they?

41. How does the Jewish understanding of religion affect this issue?

42. What were the three stages in history off the development of Christian anti-Semitism?
    Nicea

    Peter the Hermit, Martin Luther

    Hitler

43. What are some results of all this?

44. When the church did reach out to Jewish people in the past what were the two serious problems associated with how they did it?

    a.

    b.

45. So why are Jewish people closed to the Gospel?

Romans 11:1-2 (NIV)
46. Is Replacement Theology correct?

47. What is the proof that God is not done with the Jewish people?

48. Why else is it important for you to see the truth about Replacement Theology ?

49. What can you as a Gentile do?

B. Wall of Dispensational Theology

50. What is the Wall of Dispensational Theology?

Matthew 23:39

51. Is this Dispensational Theology correct?

C. Wall of Allyah-First Theology

52. What is the Wall of Aliyah-First Theology?

53. Why is this wall important?

54. Why are Jewish people from the FSU (Former Soviet Union) the most open to the Gospel ?

55. What do Christian organizations need to support?

56. Could it be God's plan to bring Jewish people to a knowledge of Yeshua in the diaspora and then bring them to Israel to bring revival to the entire nation?

57. What should I do if the Gospel isn't received the first time, even after I get past all these walls?

V. Typical Questions Jewish People Have

Colossians 4:6 ... so that you will know how to respond to any particular individual.

Use the Scriptures to answer questions.
Use the Jewish Bible because some Jewish people think Christian & Messianic Jewish translations differ from traditional Jewish translations.
Have him/her read it himself/herself.

58. When Messiah comes He is supposed to bring peace. How can Yeshua be the Messiah since the world has not had peace?

59. Aren't you either Jewish or Christian?

60. Why did God allow 6,000,000 Jews to die in the holocaust?

61. Why don't the Rabbis and the Jewish people believe in Yeshua?

62. How can Yeshua be the Son of God, or God?
   Proverbs 30:4

   Psalm 2:7

   Isaiah 9:5

63. What about all those good moral people who haven't heard?
    Romans 2:11-12

64. Does the Jewish Bible teach life after death (Heaven and Hell)?
    Daniel 12:2

    Psalm 9:18

    Job 19:26-27

65. Doesn't Isaiah 53 refer to the "Messianic Age"?

66. How can a virgin have a child?
    Isaiah 7:14

67. How can you be sure Yeshua is the Messiah?
    Daniel 9:24-25

VI. The Biggest Typical Question   69

VI. The Biggest Typical Question

68. "Don't Christians worship three gods?"

Jewish people believe there is one God.
    Monotheism was the great revelation given to Avraham.
    Judaism was the first monotheistic religion.
Christianity teaches the Trinity.
    They use names like, "Trinity Episcopal Church".
    To a Jewish observer this means they believe there are three Gods,
        therefore contradicting what Judaism teaches.
    This is especially true of Jewish people from the Western world.
    It's less true of Russians.
When Jewish people ask: don't Christians worship three Gods?
    They mean, how could I possibly consider the teachings of the Brit Hadashah
        when it clearly contradicts the Tenakh on this important point?
    Of course, the non-Messianic rabbis reinforce the confusion.

Believers usually try to resolve the apparent contradiction in ways
        that don't always help the Jewish person.

Typical explanations or proofs of the Trinity are:
- God is one God in three persons, the triune God.
    Christians go to Scriptures to prove to the Jewish person
        that there is a Holy Trinity, that God is triune in nature.
    But "Trinity" and "triune" are not words that appear in the Bible.
- The meaning of the word "Echad" in the Shema is a compound unity.
- God saying "Let us make humankind in our image" in Genesis 1:26.

    These are valid texts to show God's triune nature in the Tenakh.
    Some who teach how to share with Jewish people use these explanations.
        The problem is Jewish people interpret these three-in-one explanations to mean
          the believer is saying there are three gods
            somehow working and existing together thus contradicting the Tenakh.
        This misunderstanding can be like a veil over a Jewish person's heart
          keeping the Jewish person away from Yeshua.

Promotion of the doctrine of the Trinity in the church has been a veil for many centuries.

69. Is there a better way to address this question with Jewish people?

Let's look at what the Tenakh, the source book for Judaism, says on this subject,
and what the Brit Hadashah which, along with the Tenakh,
is the sourcebook for Christians and Messianics on this subject,
and see if they really do contradict one another,
because it is important that we know how to effectively share the truth with Jewish people.

From the Tenakh

Deuteronomy 6:4 !

70. What is this passage called and how important is it to Jewish people?

71. So, does the Tanakh teach that there is One God?

From the Brit Hadashah

Mark 12:29

72. In the Brit Hadashah, does Yeshua teach God is One?

73. What about other authors of the Brit Hadashah, like Paul?

Romans 3:30
1 Corinthians 8:6
Ephesians 4:6

First Complication:
The Brit Hadashah teaches that God is our Father.

Matthew 6:9

74. What title is God given by Yeshua?

1 Chronicles 29:10 (NKJV)

75. Is God being our Father a Brit Hadashah concept or a Tenakh concept?

Second Complication:
    The Brit Hadahah also teaches that God has a Son.

Matthew 26:63-64 (NKJV)

    76. What title does Yeshua give Himself?

Proverbs 30:4!
Psalm 2:7

    77. Is the Son of God a Brit Hadashah concept or a Tenakh concept?

But, what does it mean to be the Son of God, the Father?
    It could mean all people are God's creation, so we are all His sons.
But, it is much more because the Son has supernatural powers,
    supernatural origin, and immortality.
So, this immortal Son of God could be mistakenly seen as
    a second God alongside God the Father, which is the Jewish misconception.
        And it contradicts the Tenakh.
    But, this misconception also contradicts the Brit Hadashah.

    78. So, what does the Brit Hadashah say about the nature of the Son in the following verses?

Colossians 1:14

Colossians 1:15

Colossians 1:15-17

    79. Is the Son God Himself?

But, how does this fit with the idea that God is the invisible Father?

Philippians 2:6 .

    .

Philippians 2:7-8

So, in the Brit Hadashah, the understanding of the nature of the Father and the Son
    is that the Son is God Himself come as a man.

    80. Can you think of places in the Tenakh when God took on the form of a man?

81. So, is God taking on the form of a man a B'rit Hadashah concept or a Tenakh concept?

So, where does the confusion come in here?

Some understand that the Son come as a man as if He were separate from the Father.
   This is a natural conclusion based on several passages like this one in John where Yeshua prays to His
      Father.

John 11:41

   If one is a Father and the other His Son, they can't be the same being, can they?

John 10:30

   One God coming as a man, yet at same time existing in His invisible,
      omnipresent form is almost incomprehensible.
   It is hard for us to understand how He could do that.
      But it's certainly not impossible for God who created the universe.

Third complication
   Yeshua speaks about the Ruakh HaKodesh—Holy Spirit of God.

John 14:26
   Yeshua uses the pronoun "He," indicating the Ruakh HaKodesh is a being—has a personality.
      He is the third member of the Godhead.

   82. Does this mean there is a third God?

Remember that the Tanakh gives us further evidence of God's plurality in oneness.
Genesis 1:26
Isaiah 6:8"

   83. Who is the "us" being referred to in these two verses?

So, what does the Brit Hadashah mean?
   It seems to be contradicting itself saying God is one,
      but, there is a Son of God and a Holy Spirit of God,
         who seem to be separate from the Father God,
            yet who are also Gods, making for three Gods.

I (Rabbi Jim) have struggled with all this. Ruakh HaKodesh has given me a way to understand
   based on my background as a scientist and engineer.

The best way I have been able to understand is to realize that, as human beings,
   with limited senses and minds, we are unable to fully comprehend the fullness of God's nature.

We are unable to comprehend a being who can:
   • Communicate with billions of people at the same time.
   • Be present in the farthest reaches of the universe
      and right here simultaneously.
   • Create the laws that govern our physical universe.
   • Override those laws when He so desires.

We are unable to comprehend One who:
- Has numbered the hairs on our heads.
- Knows when a swallow dies.
- Knows each of us as individuals better than we know ourselves.

Analogy of the ants:

84. How can ants understand human nature when it is totally beyond their comprehension?

85. In the same way, how can we comprehend the fullness of God, His abilities, and His nature?

God is so wise. He knows we humans are incapable of completely understanding His nature. So, He uses things we are familiar with to teach us about His nature, and help us to appreciate Him. These things are called similes or metaphors in English. They are called models in physics and engineering.

In physics, we use models to help us understand reality. Models help us predict what the reality will do. Computers made modeling a primary tool of science and engineering.

But, we have to remember that the models are not the reality.

Analogy of the models of atom:

In the same way, God gives us descriptors of His nature.
86. He tells us He is a Father. Why a Father?

87. He tells us He is a Spirit. Why a spirit?

88. He tells us He is a Son. Why a Son?

He has also revealed Himself to us with many names—
        provider, healer, righteousness, shepherd, etc.
        These are also descriptors.
        He tells us these aspects of His nature to help us to understand
            what He is like—to the extent we as human beings
            are capable of understanding Him.

But, we must remember that in reality He is much greater than what we can conceive. Even with the help of the descriptors of His nature that He gives us. Then we don't struggle with His Triune nature not making logical sense.

We understand each descriptor as revealing one aspect of God. But we also understand that God is much more complex and more awesome than all the descriptors in every language could ever describe.

89. So, what would be the best way to answer when Jewish people ask, "Doesn't the Brit Hadashah teach there are three Gods?"

When I answered this way to Sara, her response was, "If my husband had explained it this way, I'd have become a follower of Yeshua a long time ago!"

After Jewish people receive Yeshua as their Messiah, they will come to know the Father and Son and Ruakh HaKodesh by experience.

VII. Follow up

90. What should I do after my friend receives Yeshua?

Unit Four
A Messianic
Congregation

Congregational History: Where We Came From

We came from *Beth Elohim*, *Bethel Prayer Group*, and *Chosen People*.

In 1984 we were founded by Jonathan Bernis.
   He was just out of college, was part of B'rit Hadashah Messianic Congregation.
   He was discipled by leaders in the Messianic Movement in Philadelphia and by Sid Roth.
   We met at Bethel for 4 years.
   Appel's began attending in 1984 to enable their son Jason to have a Bar Mitzvah.
   First Bar Mitzvah was in 1985.
   Appel's joined in 1986.
We were inspired to buy or build by a visit to *Beth Hallel* in Atlanta in 1987.
   We purchased Winton Road building in 1988.
Stephen and Deborah Galiley were sent out to start *Beit Shalom* in Utica.

In 1990 Jonathan Bernis visited Russia.
   He was surprised by the openness of Russian Jews.
   He felt a call to Russia.
   David Levine was brought on as assistant to free up Jonathan in 1993.
   Jonathan and teams held Festivals in Russia.
   Much follow-up was needed.
   Hear O Israel was founded and located in our building.
Goldbergs sent out to start a synagogue in Binghamton in September 1993.

David Levine became Senior Messianic Rabbi in 1994.
   Jonathan moved to St. Petersberg.
   He planted a congregation in St. Petersberg.
   His festivals continued in Moscow, Kiev, Odessa, Minsk, etc.
   Hear O Israel moved to offices in Henrietta, NY.
David and Sandy Levine were called out to oversee the planting of Russian congregations.
   David went half time in March of 1995.
   Part time staff were hired to fill in for him.
   This was evaluated in September 1995 and we decided it was not working.
   We looked for a new rabbi.

Jim Appel started as associate in March of 1996.
   Hear O Israel moved to Florida.
   Jim became Senior Rabbi in April of 1997.
Diane Robles was ordained as Pastor for Pastoral Care in June 1997.
Greenbergs were sent out to start *New Beth Israel* in Syracuse in March 1997.

We started defining our purpose December 1998.
   Our purpose Statement was completed August 2001.
Leadership Training – 2000.
Sharing Our Bread started in July 2000 (giving away groceries to the poor once a week).
   Tuesday service started for *Sharing Our Bread* people in June 2001.

Jim & Ana Copening sent out to start *Beit Emmanuel Congregation* in Naples in 2001.
Started hosting *Cleansing Stream* in February 2002 – discipling, deliverance.
David Van Slyke sent to Eugene, Oregon to start *P'nei Adonai Congregation*.
Spiritual Growth Pipeline – July 2003.
   Aleph started March 2005 – evangelism.
   Beit started July 2005 – discipleship of new believers, first level, many were Russian Jews.
   Donita Painter ordained as Administrative Pastor – 2005
   Gimmel started November 2005 – new believer discipleship, second level.
L'chaim Resource Center started 2006.
   Khavurah Group emphasis – September 2007 (small grout meeting in homes).

Revision of By-Laws – January 2008 Elders to now be elected instead of appointed.
         By-Law changes now need member approval.

First on-time budget with feedback from congregation – February 2008.
Agape Harvest – February 2008 - a food distribution program for University of Rochester graduate students, most of whom are foreign.
Danielle Howig on staff as Youth Leader – March 2008.
Election of new Elders – April 2008.
L'chaim Resource Center received non-profit status – June 2008.
Danielle Howig staff position expanded to include Children's Ministry – September 2008.
Hanukkah Outreach – December 2008.
New Shabbat School program – February 2009.

Strategic Plan – May 2009 – a plan we've been working toward.
Steady growth – 2007-2010.
Put our building up for sale – March 2010.
Revised By-laws to include congregation in final decision on sale or purchase of real estate - April 2010.
Hosted *Be In Health* Conference – May 2010.
Donita Painter moved away, Ben Rogers ordained as Assistant Messianic Rabbi - March 2011.

Congregational Life: Membership is Our Backbone

The difference between "*attenders*" and "*members*" can be summed up in one word: **Commitment**.

At CSY we recognize the need for a formal membership. We ask you to commit to membership for five reasons:

1. BIBLICAL REASON:
Eph. 5:25

2. CULTURAL REASON:

3. PRACTICAL REASON:

4. PERSONAL REASON:

5. LEGAL REASON

The Congregation is a Family

Ephesians 2:19 (LB) "...You are a member of God's very own family...and you belong in God's household with every other believer."

6. What does this verse say about the congregation?

7. "Ekklesia" (Literally: *"called out ones,"* translated *"church,"* and by us *"congregation"*) used in what two ways?
   A.

   B.

8. "Ekklesia" is only used four times in the Bible to refer to a general universal sense. Usually it is used to refer to a specific, local group of Believers. What meaning does that hold for us?

9. How important is it that you become a part of a congregation?
   A.

   B.

10. What's the difference between being a Believer and being a member of a congregation family?

What makes our congregation a family?

Four things.
- Our Salvation: What God has done for us (already covered).
- Our Purpose: Why we exist as a congregation.
- Our Strategy: How we fulfill our purpose.
- Our Organization: When and where we fulfill that purpose.

Purpose Statement: Why We Exist as a Congregation

Our Purpose Statement in a Sentence

Congregation Shema Yisrael's purposes are:

To proclaim Messiah Yeshua (Jesus) to Jewish and non-Jewish people, connect them personally with the God of Israel through prayer and worship, draw them into fellowship, lead them to spiritual maturity, equip them to serve, and inspire believers everywhere to reconnect with their Jewish roots.

Purpose Statement in Detail

(8/20/2001)

As part of the restored remnant of Israel through Messiah Yeshua, and in fulfillment of God's eternal, prophetic, providential plan at this appointed time, Congregation Shema Yisrael's purposes are:

IN EVANGELISM

to effectively and lovingly proclaim the fullness* and Jewishness of the Biblical Gospel of Messiah Yeshua, first to Jewish people, but also to the nations (non-Jewish people), locally and worldwide, and to inspire and train the non-Jewish part of Messiah's Body to effectively proclaim the Gospel to Jewish people;   (Romans 1:16-17, 1 Corinthians 9:20, Mark 16:13)

*The full Gospel includes salvation, healing, deliverance, reconciliation and immersion in the Ruakh HaKodesh (Holy Spirit) with the release of the Gifts of the Spirit.

IN FELLOWSHIP

to graft Jews and non-Jews into the Jewish root of the cultivated Olive Tree, with the bond of love, through Godly fellowship, and T'vilah (immersion in water) in order to build us into a congregation which demonstrates the One New Man in Messiah with a distinctly Messianic Jewish lifestyle and identity, and to work toward the transformation of our community through connecting in fellowship with the local Body of Messiah:
(Romans 11:16-24, Ephesians 2:15, John 17:21-22);

IN WORSHIP

to connect with the God of Israel, through His Messiah Yeshua, and glorify Him and minister to Him through worship in Spirit and Truth, as led by His Ruakh (Spirit), and especially in His Biblically appointed ways and at His Biblically appointed times, in the context of our Messianic Jewish identity;   (John 4:23-24, Leviticus 23:2)

IN PRAYER AND SPIRITUAL WARFARE

to be led by the Ruakh HaKodesh (Holy Spirit) in Spiritual Warfare against the powers of darkness and in effective prayer, for each other, our community, the lost, and the Jewish people in Israel and worldwide, to take a stand for Biblical righteousness on moral issues and against apostasy and ungodly One World Government, and to defend and support the oppressed and voiceless;
(Psalm 72:4, 12-14, 2 Thessalonians 2:7 James 1:27, Romans 8:27, Ephesians 6:12)

IN DISCIPLESHIP

to bring healing, deliverance, wholeness, the Fruit of the Spirit, spiritual maturity, a knowledge of the Jewish roots of our faith and of Messianic Jewish identity and lifestyle to God's people, including our next generation, and to equip them for service in the congregation and the Worldwide Messianic Movement, and for Aliyah, through daily Bible reading and study, solid, Spirit-led Biblical teaching, counseling, mentoring and on-the-job training;
(Ephesians 4:12-13)

IN SERVICE

to demonstrate the life of Yeshua in us and the reality of the love of God and to glorify Him through serving one another, our local community, the Body of Messiah, and the Jewish community in Israel and worldwide;   (Galatians 5:13, Matthew 5:16)

IN RESTORING THE BODY TO ITS JEWISH ROOTS

to be a bridge between the two covenantal people: physical Israel and spiritual Israel by inspiring the non-Jewish part of Messiah's Body to reconnect with its Jewish roots through Biblical teaching and worshipful demonstrations, and to work toward reconciliation between Messiah's Body and Traditional Judaism.   (Romans 11:16-24)

Our Strategy: How We Fulfill Our Purpose

SPIRITUAL GROWTH PIPELINE

After 38 years of marginally fruitful attempts of evangelizing Jewish people, we realized that something more than words is needed to remove the veil over Jewish minds and hearts.

   The veil is there because of persecution of Jews by the church.

   Humorous, yiddishkeit, artistic outreaches won't penetrate the veil.

   Matthew 5:16 In the same way, let your light shine before people, so that they may see the good things you do and praise your Father in heaven.

   This is the only way to penetrate the veil.

   We realized this is common strategy for cross cultural outreach.

      Always go to hostile cultures bringing humanitarian aid.

   Now we apply this same principle to reaching Jewish people.

THERE ARE FIVE SECTIONS TO THE SPIRITUAL GROWTH PIPELINE:

Community Outreach

   Pray to discover a need.

   Pray how to fill that need.

   Organize to meet that need with no strings attached.

   We have successfully applied this strategy through:

      Sharing Our Bread
      L'chaim Resource Center
      Hanukkah outreach, annually

Team Evangelism Strategy

   We have used Aleph Clubs

Discipleship/Mentoring – personal

   Messianic Judaism Class Group (studying this book!)

   Khavurah Groups (small groups that meet in homes)

Serving

   Sharing Our Bread

Leadership Training

   Monthly Leadership Meetings

   Khavurah Group Leaders Meetings

Pipeline undergirded by ministry teams

   Worship Team

   Dance Team

   Prayer and Spiritual Warfare Team

   Office

   Facilities Team

   Special Events

   Liturgy

Tech Team
>   R'eh Yisrael Television Ministry (local cable access)
>   Sound Team
>   Website
>   Projection
>   Network & Phones

Tikkun Olam team (missions)
Youth Group
Children's Ministries

Each ministry team may support one or more sections of the pipeline.

Principles for Rending the Veil Over Jewish Hearts

FIRST PRINCIPLE:

>   The veil is rent when a Jewish person experiences the love of God coming from those who are followers of Yeshua in a real way that touches their life. Talking and teaching about the love of God, or demonstrating it on other people will not work. Each person has to experience it themselves. Once the veil has been torn the Good News can be presented in a myriad of ways, any of which will be effective because the person will be open and seeking.

SECOND PRINCIPLE:

>   We must communicate that we are believers in Yeshua, and that our meeting of their need is inspired by the God of Israel.

THIRD PRINCIPLE:

>   We must create an environment around meeting the felt need that draws the people who are being helped to the Lord. Our goal: that people love being with us as a group and love the atmosphere that surrounds our activities and events.

FOURTH PRINCIPLE:

>   The creation of a loving environment requires a team effort—a loving, reaching out, and caring team effort.

FIFTH PRINCIPLE:

>   Teams don't just happen. They need to be built through praying together, training together, sharing a vision, having commitment and shared goals.

Our Organization: For Fulfilling Our Purpose

Congregational Government:

    The congregation is under the headship of Yeshua.

      It is governed by a Board of Elders that operates by plurality under the headship of Yeshua.

      The Senior Rabbi is the president of the Board. The elders are leaders in:

      Teaching, pastoral care, spiritual leadership, major direction setting, staffing, and budgeting.

Sample Organization chart of a Messianic Congregation

The underlined leader at the top in each box is head over the responsibilities and the leaders listed in that box. The leaders report to that underlined leader at the top. Elders on the board can be leaders of any of these teams.

<u>Senior Rabbi</u>
Shabbat Services
Messianic Judaism Class
Website content
Administrative Rabbi
Board of Elders
Khavarah Groups Head Leader
Tikkun Olam Team Leader
Sharing Our Bread Team Leader
Prayer Ministry Leader
Counseling Team Leader
Finance Team Leader
Worship Ministry Leader
Youth Leader
Children's Ministry Leader
Women's Ministry Leader

<u>Children's Ministry Leader</u>
Nursery
Shabbat School

<u>Administrative Rabbi</u>
Cantor and Liturgy
Office work
Finances:
   (banking, data entry, etc.)
L'chaim Resource Center
Community outreach
Special Events Leaders:
  Holiday celebrations, etc.
Deaf Ministry Leader
Hospitality Leader

<u>Youth Leader</u>
Junior High Youth Group
Senior High Youth Group
Youth Worship Team
Young Artists
Young Adults

<u>Worship Ministry Leader</u>
Worship Leaders
Dance Team
Tech Team
     Television Ministry
     Sound Team
     Website maintenance
     Projection
     Network & Phones

<u>Hospitality Leader</u>
Ushers
Kiddushim (refreshments)
S'udat Adonai
Facilities Team
Sermon duplication
Bookstore manager

Membership Privileges

Voice and vote
Administrative Team membership
Ministry head, Elder, Khavurah Group Leader
Counseling
Leadership assumes spiritual responsibility
Use of facility for weddings, Bar Mitzvahs
Services of Rabbi for marriages, etc.
Blessing
Bookstore discount

Membership Requirements

We never ask our members to do more than the Bible clearly teaches. We only expect our members to do what the Bible expects every Believer to do. These responsibilities are spelled out in our Membership Covenant.

Prerequisites before joining
- Age (must have completed high school)
- Born from above
- Immersed in water
- Agreement with doctrinal statement
- Involvement for six months
- Messianic Judaism Class Group (must complete this course)
- Application
- Meet with rabbi or elder
- Approved by board of elders

Requirements after joining
- Attendance
- Serving in a ministry
- Tithing
- Walking in unity, submitted to leadership
- Fellowshipping through involvement in a Khavurah Group (or involvement in a ministry of the congregation that meets this requirement)

The Philosophy which guides us in our membership requirements:

Acts 2:42-47 (NIV)
11. What key values and convictions can we draw out of this passage?

Membership Requirements in Detail

ATTENDANCE

Hebrews 10:23-25

    12. What do we learn from this Hebrews passage?

SERVING IN A MINISTRY

Matthew 20:25-28

    13. What do we learn from this Matthew passage?

Deuteronomy 10:20

    14. What do we learn from this Deuteronomy passage?

What it Means to Be a Servant

    15. Let's look at the meanings of the words "servant" and "slave."

        servant: diakonos, from diako

        slave: doulos,

These are misunderstood terms because in our American culture very few of us actually have the vocation of servant or have servants and none of us have much to do with slaves.

    16. Americans use "serve" in what three ways?

        A.

        B.

        C.

17. In the culture of the Bible what did it mean to be a servant?

18. Give two reasons why true service to God requires serving other people who are in positions of leadership in the Kingdom of God?

   A.

   B.

19. Why is true service a prerequisite for leadership within the Kingdom of God?

Serving Under Authority

Luke 7:6-10

20. What does it mean to be "under authority" and why is it important in the Kingdom of God?

Matthew 20:26-27

21. What is Yeshua telling us here?

Summary so far

22. How can you be great in God's kingdom?

Genesis 39:1-6,20-23
23. Did Yosef (Joseph) become this valued by his masters as if by magic?

Genesis 39:6,22,23

Genesis 39:3 and 23
24. What did Joseph's overseers see in him?

The Serving Principle
25. Who enables us to be good servants?

26. What happens when we are good servants?

Suppose you were in a position of responsibility like Potiphar or the jailer or you were a business owner, or a school principle, or a government administrator, or a hospital director, or a pastor in the Kingdom of God, or a Messianic Rabbi.

27. What would you look for in a person who you would be willing to put in charge of all your affairs?

Please write down all the attributes you would want.

28. Any additions?

29. Who are you serving in your life?

30. Who have you served in your congregation?

31. Look at the list you wrote down. What would the person you are serving say about your service according to the standards we came up with?

32. What does our American system of education teach about how to get ahead and be a success?

33. Does being a good performer make you a good servant?

34. Where in our education did we learn to be team players?

35. What kind of influence did the other kids in our childhoods have in discouraging us from being good servants?

36. Would you be considered someone who kisses up if you served a teacher the way we described above?

37. We've just described a powerful stronghold that greatly effects American society. It has power here because our founders were pioneers seeking to be their own bosses. It's called the _____.

38. Do these anti-servant teachings lead to success in the world?

39. What happens when you get out in the work world?

40. Does industry work on the servant principle? If so, how?

Reality in Congregations
41. What attitude do we usually have as members of congregations?

God's Plan For Serving
42. What is God's plan?

43. What is leadership's responsibility?

44. What is the people's responsibility?

45. True or false? If we all knew how to serve there would be no stopping the Kingdom of God.

46. How can you start serving?

Colossians 3:23-24 (NKJV)

TITHING AND GIVING OFFERINGS

Genesis 14:20

47. How far back does tithing go?

48. What does the word tithe mean?

Malachi 3:8-12

49. What do we learn about tithing from this passage?

50. For what will the Lord open the floodgates?

51. Where should the tithe go?

52. Can I split my tithe between congregations?

53. How is the tithe like a key?

54. How is tithing like a trust relationship?

55. Why tithe?

2 Corinthians 9:7
56. What do we learn about giving from this Corinthian passage?

57. What is the difference between a tithe and an offering?

58. Why should Messianic Jews be more inclined to tithe than Gentile believers?

Proverbs 3:9
59. Should we tithe on our net or gross income?

60. What if I cannot afford to tithe?

WALKING IN UNITY, SUBMITTED TO LEADERSHIP
Submission to leadership

Hebrews 13:17
61. How should the leaders feel who are watching over you?

62. What effect does it have on you if it is not a joy?

63. Why is it good to follow a leader's council?

Unity

Matthew 18:15-17
64. How does the Bible say we are to deal with situations in which we see others sin?

Discipline

1 Corinthians 5:1-13
65. Why was discipline enacted in Corinth?

66. How was it enacted?

67. What were the two purposes in enacting discipline?

FELLOWSHIPPING IN CHAVURAH GROUPS

John 13:34-35
68. According to Yeshua, how will the world know we are His disciples?

1 Peter 2:5
69. What image of the relationship between the believer and God's people is given here?

Galatians 6:2
70. What does bearing each other's burdens mean?

Unit Five
Statement of Faith

Congregation Shema Yisrael's Statement of Faith
(6/16/2011)

Bible

We believe that the Bible, composed of both the Tenakh and the New Covenant, is the only infallible and authoritative Word of God.
- Second Timothy 3:16, Romans 15:4, Second Peter 1:20-21, Hebrews 4:12, Ephesians 6:17

God is Echad

We believe that God is echad, as declared in the Shema, a "united one" or "compound unity", eternally existent in three persons.   - Deuteronomy 6:4, Isaiah 48:16-17, First John 5:7-11

Deity and Virgin Birth

We believe in the Deity of Yeshua HaMashiakh (Yeshua, the Messiah) and that He is the "Seed of the woman" as God promised and that His virgin birth was to be a sign to Israel of His Messiahship.   - Genesis 3:15, Isaiah 7:14, Isaiah 9:6-7, Matthew 1:22-23

Messiah Yeshua's Life

We believe in the Messiah Yeshua's life, His miracles yesterday and today, His vicarious and sacrificial death as our atonement, His bodily resurrection, His appearance thereafter in Jerusalem, His ascension, His personal future return for His followers (both living and dead), and His future establishment of His Kingdom on earth.
- Isaiah 9:6-7, Isaiah 53:8-11, Second Corinthians 5:21

Cleansed by Grace

We believe that the only means of being saved from sin and iniquity is by God's grace, through faith in the shed sacrificial blood of Yeshua HaMashiach, and that regeneration by the Spirit of God is absolutely essential for personal salvation.
- Leviticus 17:11, Ephesians 2:8, Romans 1:17

Ruakh HaKodesh

We believe in the present ministry of the Ruach HaKodesh (Holy Spirit) by whose indwelling the believer is enabled to live a Godly life.   - Jeremiah 31:31-34, John 14:15-17, Galatians 3:13-25

Resurrection

We believe in the resurrection of both the saved and lost, the one to everlasting life and the other to eternal separation from God, the latter being a state of everlasting punishment.
- Daniel 12:2, Matthew 25:46, Genesis 15:6

Sons and Daughters of Israel

We believe that the Jews (descendents of Jacob, whether through the blood line of mothers or fathers) who place their faith in Israel's Messiah have not disowned or separated themselves from their race and Judaic heritage, but remain sons and daughters of Israel. Gentiles who place their faith in Israel's Messiah are also, spiritually, sons and daughters of Israel.
- Galatians 3:28-29, Romans 2:28-29

Middle Wall of Partition

We believe that the middle wall of partition which in times past separated Jews and Gentiles has been broken down, the enmity between them eradicated by the Messiah Yeshua.

- Ephesians 2:12-24, Acts 10:34

New Covenant Body

We believe that the New Covenant body of the Lord is composed of both Jews and Gentiles who have accepted Yeshua as the promised Redeemer, and that now they are to worship together in the House of God.

- First Corinthians 12:13, Hebrews 10:25

Jewish Followers of Yeshua

We believe that as Jewish followers of Yeshua, we are called to maintain our Jewish Biblical heritage and remain a part of our people, Israel, and the universal body of believers. This is part of our identity and a witness to the faithfulness of God.

- Romans 3:1-4, First Corinthians 7:17-18, Acts 21:20-24

Marriage

We believe that marriage is a holy estate, ordained by God to be entered into by one man and one woman.

-Genesis 2:20-24

Homosexuality

We believe that homosexuality is an abomination to God. God loves all people, including those who practice homosexuality, and we seek to demonstrate His love to them and plead with them to turn from this abomination and receive His forgiveness. But none who continue in their practice of this abomination can be members, employees, or hold positions of leadership in this congregation.

-Leviticus 18:22, 20:13

Congregation Shema Yisrael's Statement of Faith, in detail

THE BIBLE
(6/18/2011)

We believe that the Bible, composed of both the Tenakh (Old Covenant) and the Apostolic Writings of the New Covenant (Brit Hadasha) is the only infallible and authoritative Word of God.

2 Timothy 3:15-17

1. What writings do the "Holy Scriptures" include?

2. What does the word "Scripture" mean?

3. What are the purposes of the Scriptures?

4. What does God-breathed mean?

Romans 15:4

5. What does the "everything" refer to?

6. What additional purposes of the Scripture are given here?

2 Peter 1:16-21

7. What incident is Peter referring to when he speaks of the voice?

8. What does Peter mean by "we have the prophetic Word made very certain"?
   (NKJV verse 19 And so we have the prophetic Word confirmed,)

9. Where do the prophecies in Scripture come from?

10. How do we know that the prophecies in Scripture came from God?

God has put a proof-test in the Bible that He spoke it.

Deuteronomy 18:22
   11. What is the test of a prophet?

   12. What can we infer about a prophet if his predictions come true?

Here's a sampling of already fulfilled prophecies
   Use them to defend your belief that the Bible is the Word of God. When witnessing to someone Jewish, give them the following already fulfilled prophecies relating to the Jewish people.

Words written by Moses in the desert, 1520-1400 BCE

Deuteronomy 29:23-28
   13. What is being described?

   14. When did it start?

Other words written by Moses in the desert, 1520-1400 BCE

Deut. 28:63-67 .
   15. What is being described?

   16. When did it start?

More words written by Moses in the desert, 1520-1400 BCE

Deuteronomy 30:2-4
   17. What is being described here?

   18. When did it start?

Words written by Isaiah in 783-704 BCE

Isaiah 27:6
    19. What is being described here?

    20. Who supplies Europe with citrus fruit?

    21. When did it start?

Words of Jeremiah 626-586 BCE

Jeremiah 16:14-15
    22. What is being described here?

    23. When did it happen?

Words of Jeremiah 626-586 BCE

Jeremiah 31:35-37
    24. What is being described here?

    25. When did it happen?

Words of Zechariah 550 BCE

Zech 12:2-3
    26. What is being described here?

    27. When did it happen?

28. According to the traditional Jewish interpretation of Exodus 20:1-17 (NKJV), what are the Ten Commandments or "Words" from God? (In Hebrew, they are called the "Ten Words" or "Sayings.")

I.

II.

III.

IV.

V.

VI.

VII.

VIII.

IX.

X.

29. According to Mark 12:28-34, what are the two greatest commandments? Where are they found in the Tenakh?

30. What do many Christians call the Tenakh?

31. What does B'rit Hadashah mean?

GOD IS ECHAD אחד

(6/21/2011)

We believe that God is "Echad", as described in the Shema "a united one" or "compound unity" eternally existent in three persons as expressed in Isaiah 48:16 and 1 John 5:7-11.

Isaiah 48:16

32. Who is the me who has spoken since the beginning?

Deuteronomy 6:4 Hear, O Israel: The LORD our God, the LORD is one.

From the *Strong's Concordance:*

H259. 'echad, ekh-awd'; a numeral from H258; prop. united, i.e. one; or (as an ordinal) first:--a, alike, alone, altogether, and, any (-thing), apiece, a certain [dai-] ly, each (one), + eleven, every, few, first, + highway, a man, once, one, only, other, some, together.

H3173. yachiyd, yaw-kheed'; from H3161; prop. united, i.e. sole; by impl. beloved; also lonely: (fem.) the life (as not to be replaced):--darling, desolate, only (child, son), solitary.

Genesis 1:26

33. Who is the "us" being referred to here?

As we learned earlier, Jewish people believe that the Brit Hadashah teaches that there are three gods somehow working and existing together thus contradicting the Tenakh.
This misunderstanding keeps many Jewish people away from Yeshua.

This is discussed in depth in the Jewish Evangelism unit beginning with question #68 (p. 67).

DEITY AND VIRGIN BIRTH

(6/19/2011)

We believe in the Deity of Yeshua HaMashiakh (Yeshua, the Messiah) and that He is the "Seed of the woman" as God promised and that His virgin birth was to be a sign to Israel of His Messiahship.

DEITY

Isaiah 9:6-7

34. How will the Messiah come?

35. Is He just a man?

36. How long has He been around?

37. How long will He be around?

38. Where has He reigned since He came?

Acts 14:13-15
Revelations 19:9-10

39. What happened when men tried to worship other men or an angel?

Matthew 28:9-10

40. What happened when the women worshipped Yeshua?

41. Who do we conclude Yeshua is from these passages?

Colossians 1:15-19

42. What does God look like? (Verse 15)

43. What did Yeshua have to do with the process of creation? (Verse 16)

44. What kind of "thrones, powers, rulers or authorities" are being referred to here?

45. Who holds everything together?

46. Who is the head of the body? (Verse 18)

47. What does it mean that Yeshua is the "beginning"?

48. Who was the first to be resurrected?

49. What does it mean that He has supremacy in everything?

50. How much of God dwells in Yeshua? (Verse 19)

Hebrews 1:2-3
51. In what way did God make the universe?

52. What does "the radiance of the Sh'kinah" mean?

53. What does "the very expression of God's essence" mean?

54. What upholds or sustains all that exists?

Philippians 2:5-12
55. What form was Yeshua in prior to coming to earth?

56. What does it mean to be equal to God?

VIRGIN BIRTH
Matthew 1:22-23
57. What prophesy is Matthew quoting?

Isaiah 7:14 (NKJV)
The Hebrew word is "Almah" H5959 עלמה "*a lass (as veiled or private); —damsel, maid, virgin.*" (See CJB Commentary to Matthew 1:23.) Matthew is quoting the Septuagint which is a Greek translation of the Tanakh, translated 250 years before Yeshua. It was translated by Jewish translators. They chose the Greek word "parthenos" which means "virgin".

58. What does "Immanuel" mean?

MESSIAH YESHUA'S LIFE

(6/19/2011))

We believe in Messiah Yeshua's life, His miracles yesterday and today, His vicarious and sacrificial death as our atonement, His bodily resurrection, His appearance thereafter in Jerusalem, His ascension, His personal future return for His followers, (both living and dead), and His future establishment of His Kingdom on Earth.

Isaiah 9:6-7

59. What kingdom's government will be upon His shoulders?

60. Has the dominion extended (KJV increased) and peace been perpetuated (KJV increased)?

61. Has there been a king reigning on David's physical throne?

62. If Yeshua had not come when He did would this prophesy be true?

63. What does "vicarious" mean in the statement of faith?

64. What does "atonement" mean in the statement of faith?

Isaiah 53:4-11 (NKJV)

65. What phrases in the statement of faith are supported by this passage?

66. What does the word "esteemed" mean in verse 4?

67. What are the "iniquities" in verse 5?

68. What does "chastisement" mean in verse 5?

The sinless man made a sin offering:

> *2 Corinthians 5:21 (NIV) God made Him who had no sin to be sin* for us, so that in Him we might become the righteousness of God.*

Scapegoat passage:

> *Leviticus 16:21-22 Aharon (Aaron) is to lay both his hands on the head of the live goat and confess over it all the transgressions, crimes and sins of the people of Isra'el; he is to put them on the head of the goat and then send it away into the desert with a man appointed for the purpose. 22 The goat will bear all their transgressions away to some isolated place, and he is to let the goat go in the desert.*

Yeshua is our Scapegoat:

> *Isaiah 53:6 (NKJV) We all, like sheep, have gone astray, each of us has turned to his own way; and the LORD has laid on Him the iniquity of us all.*

1 Corinthians 15:1-8
69. What part of the statement of faith does this passage address?

70. How many people who had seen Yeshua resurrected were still alive when this was written?

Acts 1:9-11
71. How did He leave?

72. How will He return?

Luke 22:29-30
73. Who will sit on these thrones?

CLEANSED BY GRACE

(6/16/2011)

We believe that the only means of being cleansed from sin is by grace, through faith in the shed sacrificial blood of Yeshua HaMashiach, and that regeneration by the Spirit of God is absolutely essential for personal salvation.

Leviticus 17:8-11

74. What is required to make atonement for sin?

75. Where can the offerings or sacrifices be made?

76. What happened in 70 CE that affected this way of dealing with sin?

77. What provision did God make to deal with this event?

78. What change did Traditional Judaism make to deal with this event?

Ephesians 2:8-9

79. What is the difference between trust (or faith) and intellectual assent?

80. What kind of trust is this verse referring to?

81. How much work do you have to do to receive this gift?

Romans 1:17

82. What is righteousness?

John 3:3 "Yes, indeed," Yeshua answered him, "I tell you that unless a person is born again from above, he cannot see the Kingdom of God."

83. What does it mean to be "born again from above"?

RUAKH HAKODESH

(6/19/2011)

We believe in the present ministry of the Ruach HaKodesh (Holy Spirit) by whose indwelling the believer is enabled to live a godly life.

The present ministry of the Ruakh HaKodesh

Acts 1:8

84. What do you receive when the Ruach HaKodesh comes upon you?

85. What is God's purpose in giving us the Ruach HaKodesh?

86. What is the evidence that the Ruach HaKodesh has come upon a person?

87. Must you speak in tongues to be filled with the Ruach HaKodesh?

Luke 23:42-43

88. Do you need to be filled with the Ruach HaKodesh to be saved?

Romans 8:14.

89. What role of the Ruach HaKodesh is mentioned here?

John 16:13-14

90. What role of the Ruach HaKodesh is mentioned here?

Romans 8:26-27

91. What role of the Ruach HaKodesh is mentioned here?

John 14:16 "and I will ask the Father, and he will give you another comforting Counselor like me, the Spirit of Truth, to be with you forever."
(NKJV) "And I will pray the Father, and He will give you another Helper, that He may abide with you forever.
(NIV) "And I will ask the Father, and he will give you another Counselor to be with you forever."

92. What roles of the Ruach HaKodesh are mentioned here?

1 Corinthians 12:7
93. What does the Spirit give us?

Galatians 5:22
94. What does the Spirit produce in our lives?

CONNECTION TO TENAKH

Acts 2:1 The festival of Shavu'ot arrived, and the believers all gathered together in one place.

(KJV) When the Day of Pentecost had fully come, they were all with one accord in one place.

Leviticus 23:15-17

Exodus 19:1

95. Why were the believers in Acts 2 gathered in one place at sunrise?

Acts 2:2-4.
96. What phrase is used to describe this encounter with the Ruach HaKodesh?

97. What gift of the Spirit accompanied their receiving the Ruach HaKodesh?

98. What are the parallels with Sinai?

Acts 2:5-8
99. What purpose did the "different languages" serve?

Acts 10:44-46
100. How did the Jewish believers know the Gentiles had received the Ruach HaKodesh?

Acts 10:47-48
   101. What purpose did the speaking in tongues serve?

   102. What is the order of immersions here?

Acts 19:1-2
   103. What was Rabbi Sha'ul's (Paul's) first concern when he met these new believers?

Acts 19:6
   104. What did the Ephesians do when they were immersed in the Ruach?

1 Corinthians 14:4
   105. What purpose did the speaking in tongues and prophesying serve?

Acts 2:4
   106. Who spoke?

   107. What does "as the Spirit gave them utterance" (KJV) or "enabled them to speak" mean?

Acts 2:38
   108. What are the requirements for receiving the gift of the Ruach HaKodesh?

Luke 11:9-13
   109. If we ask for the Ruach HaKodesh, what will God do?

   110. What are you to conclude if you don't feel any different?

Ephesians 5:18-21
   111. Are we exhorted to do the activities just once or continually?

SONS AND DAUGHTERS OF ISRAEL

(6/21/2011)

We believe that the Jews according to the flesh (descendants of Abraham through Isaac, whether through the blood line of the mother or the father) who place their faith in Israel's Messiah Yeshua have not disowned or separated themselves from their race and Judaic heritage, but remain sons and daughters of Israel. Gentiles who place their faith in Israel's Messiah Yeshua are also, spiritually sons and daughters of Israel.

Jewish People Remain Sons and Daughters of Israel

Genesis 46:8-27

112. How does this first genealogy of the Children of Israel relate to the parenthetical statement in the statement of faith?

113. Why do traditional Jews reckon genealogy through the mother?

Acts 20:16

114. What's the Hebrew name for Pentecost?

Deuteronomy 16:16

115. Why did Rabbi Sha'ul need to be in Jerusalem for Shavuot?

Acts 28:17

116. What did Rabbi Sha'ul continue to keep in addition to the law after he became a believer?

Acts 21:20

Early Jewish followers of Yeshua did not disown or separate themselves from their race and Judaic heritage, but remained sons and daughters of Israel.

Gentiles

Ephesians 2:11-12
    117. What do other translations use for "national life of Israel?

Ephesians 2:12-19

    118. What position does this passage give Gentile believers?

    119. What happened to turn this understanding upside down in our world today?

Romans 11:16
    120. Who is the root?

Romans 11:17-18
    121. Who are the broken off branches?

    122. Who is the grafted-in wild olive shoot?

    123. Whom does who nourish?

Romans 11:18b
    124. Who supports who?

Romans 11:19-20
    125. Who is being warned & what are they being warned about?

Romans 11:21
>   126. What happened over the next 300 years?

    In Shaul's day there were:
      Congregations of Messianic Jews in Israel.
      Congregations of Jews and Gentiles in Diaspora.
      Messianic Jewish Leadership in Jerusalem.
    Rome destroyed Israel from 70 - 135 ACE. Surviving Jewish people were dispersed throughout the Roman Empire and persecuted.
      The Jewish leadership of Messiah's body was dispersed.
      There was great persecution of Jewish and Gentile believers by the Romans.
    The Gospel spread throughout the Roman Empire.
      People thought Judaism would disappear.
          Replacement Theology took over—The Church was the New Israel
              It was a very nice, self satisfying theology that made them feel good and important.
              They became very attached to it.
    Gentile leadership increased because the number of Gentiles in the Body increased.
    But, non-Messianic Judaism did not disappear. It flourished in the Roman Empire, contradicting Replacement Theology, and competing with Messianic Jews for the hearts of Jewish people.
    The existence of non-Messianic Jews was an affront to the theologians.
          They couldn't live with it.
          It refuted their self image of being God's chosen people.
          So, they began to hate Judaism which led to hatred of non-Messianic Jews and cutting off the church from its Jewish roots.
    Also, because of persecution of Jews by Rome, Gentile believers did not want to be identified as Jews.
    Around 300 ACE Roman Emperor, Constantine, became a believer.
          He took over the Body of Messiah at the Council of Nicea.
          He ended persecution of the believers.
    He turned the Body from a Jewish movement to a Roman military structure.
    The church leadership outlawed Jewish practice within the Body.

>   127. What happened to the olive tree in Romans 11?

Daniel 4:15
>   128. What happened to the root (or stump)?

129. What happened to the world?

For hundreds of years, the Dark Ages prevailed.

The Reformation was a break in this branch's power. Branches broke away from the Catholic tree. But, instead of going back to the root and grafting themselves in, the broken off branches also planted themselves in the ground. Other branches broke off and also planted themselves in the ground.

The result: continuous division as new branches seek the sap they need and can't find it because they have no root.

They're designed to be branches, not roots.

The sap only comes from the root which is Yeshua and Messianic Judaism.

This is a deep, strong root which the wild branches are meant to be grafted into.

This is an ongoing offense by the Gentile Church against Messianic Jews:

Outlawing of Jewish practices:

Shabbat, Feasts of the Lord, Rosh Kodesh, Jubilee, and Kashrut.

The Gentile church is turning toward repentance of anti-Semitic treatment of Jews. But they're not aware that the root of anti-Semitism is the breaking off of the branches from the Jewish root.

If the Church had maintained its Jewish roots, how could it have become anti-Semitic?

They're not aware that the root cause of the division within the church is the breaking off of the branches from the Jewish root.

Rom 11:22-24

130. How can Messiah's Body get re-connected to the root?

131. How is God re-grafting in the broken off branches?

He's removing the iron and bronze bands from the root to enable the stump to sprout again.

He's causing Messianic Judaism to flourish.

He is awakening in Gentile believers a hunger for an understanding of their Jewish roots.

He's bringing new revelation in the Gentile Church:

God is still interested in Appointed Times for the entire body.

They want to know how to worship according to God's Appointed Times and ways.

We Messianic Jews are receiving a deeper understanding of His Appointed Times (Moadim). (See p. 26.)

He's bringing a spirit of repentance to the Gentile church:
• for its treatment of Jews.
• for cutting itself off from its Jewish roots.

How God is re-grafting (continued list)

Examples of God doing these things in our midst:

(Usually with a surprise of more than expected from the Lord.)

Messiah Conferences

The attendance is increasing and increasing.

Gentile pastors led by John Dawson in 1997 repented before the entire assembly for their treatment of Jewish people and for cutting off from their Jewish roots.

Standing In The Gap

The intention was repentance for the USA.

In 1997, it was scheduled for Shabbat T'shuvah, the Sabbath of Repentance, without a clue as to its significance.

Messianic Jews explained it to the leadership.

Surprise: Shofars and Marty Waldman's prayer broke it open.

Jewish knowledge of a Moadim was received.

Shavuot

We were invited to demonstrate the significance of one of God's Moadim: Shavuot.

Surprise: Resulted in the newspaper article which enabled us to proclaim His Word.

Jewish knowledge of a Moadim was received.

Budapest

Outreach to Jews.

Surprise: Repentance of the church for treatment of Jews.

Prayer and Spiritual Warfare Conference

Jewish knowledge of a Moadim was received.

Blowing the Jubilee Shofar

A Church in Rochester received the Jubilee blessing from us.

Surprise: Repentance and prayer for revival of Jewish people.

132. What is our role as Messianic Jews in this re-grafting?

- To teach the truth to the church about its Jewish roots.
- To participate in reconciliation.
- To pray for church to repent about treatment of Jewish people for their sake and ours.
- To pray for church to repent for breaking itself off from and not yet going back to its Jewish roots.
- To lead in worship.
- To bring the restoration of dance.
- To serve during God's Moadim:
    Shabbat, Rosh Khodesh (New Moon), Biblical Holidays.
        Gentiles don't know how to keep these days.

John Dawson's message:

- Messianic Jews are the elder brother.
- Messianic Jews have reached the point where we are no longer struggling just to survive.
- We are beginning to intercede for the rest of the body.
- We all need a lot of prayer.

(John Dawson is president of YWAM and part of the International Reconciliation Coalition founded in 1990.)

Old and New Covenants

Hebrews 8:13 By using the term, "new," he has made the first covenant "old"; and something being made old, something in the process of aging, is on its way to vanishing altogether.

Jewish New Testament Commentary – by David H. Stern (page 691)
By using the term, "new," he has made the first covenant "old." The author *[of Hebrews]* is not criticizing the Mosaic Covenant but merely making explicit what Jeremiah implied. Sha'ul had already used the phrase, "Old Covenant," at 2 Cor. 3:14.

Is one to infer that the Jewish holidays, *Shabbat, kashrut*, civil laws, and moral laws of the Mosaic Covenant are on the verge of vanishing altogether? No, for the author could hardly have been unaware that the Mosaic Covenant presents itself as eternal; also the context shows that he is speaking only of its system of priests and sacrifices, not its other aspects. Since the laws concerning the cultus *[sacrificial system]* constitute the majority of the Mosaic prescriptions, it is not an inappropriate figure of speech to say that the Old Covenant itself is aging and about to disappear.

In this verse, the verb tenses are important. The Mosaic Covenant has already been **made ... old,** but it is not already aged and it has not already vanished. It is **in the process of aging** and **on the verge of vanishing** in the same sense that "This world's leaders ... are in the process of passing away" (2C 2:6). This world's leaders are still with us, and so is the Mosaic Covenant. Even Christians whose theology posits the abrogation or passage of the Mosaic Covenant in its entirety must therefore acknowledge that it has not yet vanished but still exists. Some have inferred from this language that at the time the author wrote, the Temple was still standing and the author was predicting what Yeshua had already prophesied (Mt 24:2, Mk 13:2, Lk 21:2), that the Temple would soon be destroyed by the Romans in 70 c.e., at which time the sacrifices would cease and the priesthood would be left without work to do. This is a possible interpretation, although against it is the fact that the author never refers to the Temple but always to the Tent (Tabernacle), which had passed out of existence a thousand years earlier. ... No matter when the author wrote, his arguments do provide a rationale for Messianic Jews not to be distressed by the passing of the Temple and to carry on anyhow; in this sense, the role of the book of Messianic Jews is comparable with that of the Yavneh Council in non-Messianic Judaism (c. 90 c.e.), which transferred its focus from the Temple to the Written and Oral Torah. The book instructs Messianic Jews to center not on the Temple but on the Messiah and what he has done.

What is actually on the verge of vanishing is the old priesthood, not the old covenant—or, perhaps we may say, not God's unchangeable nature which stands behind the old covenant. The priesthood is the subject of the whole section (indeed, the sacrificial system is the subject of the whole letter), and it is this which is about to disappear or, at the very least, take on a very much transformed role.... On this verse Paul Ellingworth, who has also written a commentary on Hebrews, says: "This refers to the replacement of the old cult *[sacrificial system]* by the new, not to a change in the ethical or civil requirements of the Torah!" The "old" Torah continues, and continues to have its same purpose, but there is now a new system of cohanim, as has already been said and will be explained further in the next two chapters *[of Hebrews]*.
Jewish New Testament Commentary © 1989, by David H. Stern
published by Jewish New Testament Publications, Inc.

RESURRECTION

(6/19/2011)

We believe in the resurrection of both saved and lost, the one to everlasting life and the other to eternal separation from God, the latter being consigned to a state of everlasting punishment

Daniel 12:2

133. Who shall be resurrected?

134. What two states of being await those who will be resurrected?

135. How long is everlasting?

olam; *time out of mind (past or future), i.e., (practically) eternity; freq. adv. (espec. with prep. pref.) always:--always (-s), ancient (time), any more, continuance, eternal, (for, [n-]) ever (-lasting, -more, of old), lasting, long (time), (of) old (time), perpetual, at any time, (beginning of the) world (+ without end).*

Matthew 25:46

aionios, ahee-o'-nee-os; *perpetual (also used of past time, or past and future as well):* —*eternal, forever, everlasting, world (began)*

John 11:25-26

136. What two things may happen to those who believe in Yeshua?

137. What kind of death is referred to here?

138. What kind of life?

I Corinthians 15:3-6

139. What evidence is there in this verse of the truth of the Resurrection?

1 Corinthians15:49

140. With what kind of body will we be resurrected?

MIDDLE WALL OF PARTITION

(6/19/2011)

We believe that the middle wall of partition that in times past separated Jews and Gentiles has been broken down, the enmity between them eradicated by the Messiah Yeshua.

Ephesians 2:14 For he himself is our shalom—he has made us both one and has broken down the m'chitzah [dividing wall of hostility] which divided us.

141. What is the purpose of the m'chitzah?

Ephesians 2:15 ... by destroying in His own body the enmity occasioned by the Torah, with its commands set forth in the form of ordinances. He did this in order to create in union with himself from the two groups a single new humanity and thus make shalom.

142. How did He destroy the m'chitzah?

143. How did the Torah "occasion" enmity between Jews and Gentiles?

144. How do other English translations translate this verse?

Ephesians 2:15 (NIV) **by abolishing in his flesh the law with its commandments and regulations.** *His purpose was to create in himself one new man out of the two, thus making peace.*

145. Do you see a problem with this translation?

Matthew 5:17-19 "Don't think that I have come to abolish the Torah or the Prophets. I have come not to abolish but to complete. 18 Yes indeed! I tell you that until heaven and earth pass away, not so much as a yud or a stroke will pass from the Torah—not until everything that must happen has happened. 19 So whoever disobeys the least of these mitzvot and teaches others to do so will be called the least in the Kingdom of Heaven. But whoever obeys them and so teaches will be called great in the Kingdom of Heaven."

146. Was the law (Torah) destroyed or the "enmity occasioned by the Torah" destroyed?

Ephesians 2:16 (CJB and NKJV)

147. What was put to death?

Ephesians 2:17
   148. Who was nearby and who was far off?

Ephesians 2:13
   149. Who has now been brought near?

Ephesians 2:18-19
   150. What status do the Gentiles have?

Ephesians 2:20-22
   151. How can we apply the analogy used here to each group's need for the other?

NEW COVENANT BODY

(6/19/2011)

We believe that the New Covenant Body of the Lord is composed of both Jews and Gentiles who have accepted Yeshua HaMashiach as the promised redeemer and that now they are to worship TOGETHER in the House of God

1 Corinthians 12:12-13

152. What does the use of a human body as an analogy here suggest about the relationship of Jews and Gentiles in the body or mishpokhah (family)?

153. What is the effect on the body's ability to function if a part of it is missing?

Ephesians 3:4

154. When was the "secret plan (or mystery) concerning the Messiah" made known?

Ephesians 3:5-6

155. What is this "secret plan (or mystery)" of the Messiah?

156. What does the word "joint" imply?

157. Why does Rabbi Sha'ul use "joint" three times?

Ephesians 3:9-10

158. God's intent is that His wisdom in this mystery be made known to whom?

159. Who informs them?

160. How are we supposed to inform them?

161. What does our informing them imply?

JEWISH FOLLOWERS OF YESHUA

(6/19/2011)

We believe that Jewish followers of Yeshua are called to maintain their Jewish Biblical heritage and remain a part of Israel, and the universal body of believers. This is part of our identity and a witness to the faithfulness of God.

Romans 3:1-2

162. What have the Jewish people been entrusted with?

Romans 3:3-4

163. God's faithfulness is being affirmed relative to what?

1 Corinthians 7:17-18

164. What point is Rabbi Sha'ul trying to make here?

165. How would Rabbi Sha'ul view a Jewish person who stopped living a Jewish lifestyle when they decided to believe in Messiah?

Acts 21:20

166. Who did these thousands believe in?

167. What does it mean that they were zealots for the Torah?

Acts 21:21

168. Who was being accused?

169. What was he being accused of?

Acts 21:22-24

170. Was the accusation about Rabbi Sha'ul true?

171. How did they attempt to prove it was not true?

Watch or listen to sermons by Rabbi Jim:

www.shemayisrael.org

Buy this or other books by Rabbi Jim:

www.olivepresspublisher.org
or
www.olivepresspublisher.com

To watch Rabbi Jonathan Bernis:

www.jewishvoice.org

CPSIA information can be obtained
at www.ICGtesting.com
Printed in the USA
LVHW060339140421
684459LV00008B/36